Personal Reflections
on Counseling

Gerald Corey

AMERICAN COUNSELING
ASSOCIATION

6101 Stevenson Avenue, Suite 600 • Alexandria, VA 22304
www.counseling.org

Personal Reflections
on Counseling

American Counseling Association
6101 Stevenson Avenue, Suite 600 • Alexandria, VA 22304

Associate Publisher • Carolyn C. Baker

Digital and Print Development Editor • Nancy Driver

Senior Production Manager • Bonny E. Gaston

Copy Editor • Kay Mikel

Cover and text design by Bonny E. Gaston.

Library of Congress Cataloging-in-Publication Data

Names: Corey, Gerald, author.
Title: Personal reflections on counseling / Gerald Corey.
Description: Alexandria, VA : American Counseling Association, [2020] | Includes bibliographical references.
Identifiers: LCCN 2019056240 | ISBN 9781556203954 (paperback)
Subjects: LCSH: Counseling—Vocational guidance. | Counseling psychology—Vocational guidance.
Classification: LCC BF636.64 .C673 2020 | DDC 158.3—dc23
LC record available at https://lccn.loc.gov/2019056240

Dedication

*To students and new professionals,
may you be inspired to create and follow
your own personal and professional paths.*

Table of Contents

Preface

For many years, I have been giving presentations at American Counseling Association conferences, including a program titled "Becoming a Professional Counselor: For Graduate Students and New Professionals." The attendees ask many questions about navigating a counseling career and balancing their personal life with a professional life. I decided to write this book to reach out to a larger audience beyond these annual meetings. In preparation for writing this book, I asked a number of my colleagues and students to provide questions for my consideration, and I added questions I wanted to address as well. Many of the topics will be familiar and appear in books I have authored or coauthored, but the thematic context is unique and addresses a broad range of issues. I hope this book will be an inspiration to counselors who are just beginning their personal and professional journey.

In *Personal Reflections on Counseling*, I share my insights and the lessons I have learned over my 60-year career in the counseling profession. I engage in considerable self-disclosure on a wide variety of topics, and I hope this will encourage readers to engage in an active process of self-reflection that is useful both personally and professionally. As I was writing, I imagined myself talking with my students, and I strived to be concise, practical, and personal. I view this book as a mentoring endeavor, providing suggestions, recommendations, and advice on a wide range of subjects.

Topics addressed include creating your professional path, mentoring and being a mentee, surviving graduate school and beyond, reviewing changes in the counseling profession, benefiting from your personal therapy, focusing on self-care and wellness, becoming an ethical counselor, managing value conflicts in counseling, using self-disclosure therapeutically, dealing with difficult clients, getting the most out of supervision, and becoming a writer. At the end of each chapter, Reflection Questions ask you to engage in thinking about and applying these topics to yourself.

This book is a valuable supplement for a variety of courses in counseling, counselor education, human services, psychology, and social work; and its candid prose will delight students taking an introduction to the counseling profession, practicum, or internship course. I expect the book to have special relevance for graduate students (on both the master's and doctoral levels) and new professionals.

Acknowledgments

I greatly appreciate the constructive feedback I received from colleagues and former students who reviewed the manuscript and encouraged me to keep this book personal and inspirational. Marianne Schneider Corey, my wife and colleague, did an amazing job of keeping me on track, keeping me honest, and suggesting ways to introduce personal experiences in a relevant and effective manner. We had many productive discussions throughout this project, and her insights have added depth to the answers explored in the book. Others who reviewed the manuscript, suggested additional ideas, and offered valuable input to enhance the discussion are:

- Jude T. Austin II, PhD, the University of Mary Hardin-Baylor
- Julius A. Austin, PhD, Tulane University
- Jamie Bludworth, PhD, Arizona State University
- Amanda Connell, MS, California State University at Fullerton
- Robert Haynes, PhD, clinical psychologist and former director of training at Atascadero State Hospital
- Barbara Herlihy, PhD, University of Texas at San Antonio
- Dianne Mason, graduate student in counseling, California State University at Fullerton
- Jeremy Rintalan, graduate student in social work, California State University at Fullerton

Special appreciation goes to Carolyn Baker, the associate publisher at the American Counseling Association. Carolyn contributed her expertise by reviewing the manuscript, providing helpful comments and suggestions for consistency in style, and offering support throughout the writing and revision process. A special thank you goes to our manuscript editor Kay Mikel, whose editorial talents ensured a personal and practical presentation. Producing a book is truly a team effort, and both Carolyn and Kay, along with all of the reviewers, are key people on this team, and I thank them one and all.

About the Author

Gerald Corey, EdD, ABPP, is professor emeritus of human services and counseling at California State University at Fullerton. He received his doctorate in counseling in 1967 from the University of Southern California. He was awarded an honorary doctorate in Humane Letters in 1992 from National Louis University. He is a Diplomate in Counseling Psychology, American Board of Professional Psychology; a licensed psychologist in California; and a National Certified Counselor. He is a Fellow of the American Psychological Association (Division 17, Counseling Psychology; and Division 49, Group Psychotherapy); a Fellow of the American Counseling Association; and a Fellow of the Association for Specialists in Group Work. In addition to these organizations, he holds memberships in the American Group Psychotherapy Association, the Association for Counselor Education and Supervision, the Western Association of Counselor Education and Supervision, and the National Organization for Human Services. He received the Lifetime Achievement Award from the American Mental Health Counselors Association in 2011, the Eminent Career Award from Association for Specialists in Group Work in 2001, and the Outstanding Professor of the Year Award from California State University at Fullerton in 1991. He teaches courses in theories of counseling, group counseling, and ethics in counseling. He is the author or coauthor of 16 textbooks in counseling currently in print, along with more than 70 journal articles and numerous book chapters. His book *Theory and Practice of Counseling and Psychotherapy* has been translated into Arabic, Indonesian, Portuguese, Turkish, Korean, and Chinese. *Theory and Practice of Group Counseling* has been translated into Korean, Chinese, Spanish, and Russian. *Issues and Ethics in the Helping Professions* has been translated into Korean, Japanese, and Chinese. With his colleagues, he has conducted workshops in the United States, Germany, Ireland, Belgium, Scotland, Mexico, Canada, China, and Korea—with a special focus on training participants in group counseling. He has presented workshops for professional organizations and special intensive courses at various universities.

The following seven Corey books are published by the American Counseling Association:

- *Clinical Supervision in the Helping Professions: A Practical Guide*, Third Edition (2021, with Robert Haynes, Patrice Moulton, and Michelle Muratori)
- *Personal Reflections on Counseling* (2020)
- *The Art of Integrative Counseling*, Fourth Edition (2019)
- *Counselor Self-Care* (2018, with Michelle Muratori, Jude T. Austin, and Julius A. Austin II)
- *ACA Ethical Standards Casebook*, Seventh Edition (2015, with Barbara Herlihy)
- *Boundary Issues in Counseling: Multiple Roles and Relationships*, Third Edition (2015, with Barbara Herlihy)
- *Creating Your Professional Path: Lessons from My Journey* (2010)

Recent publications by Gerald Corey and colleagues with Cengage Learning include:

- *Becoming a Helper*, Eighth Edition (2021, with Marianne Schneider Corey)
- *Theory and Practice of Counseling and Psychotherapy*, Enhanced Tenth Edition (2021, and *Student Manual*, 2017)
- *Issues and Ethics in the Helping Professions*, Tenth Edition (2019, with Marianne Schneider Corey and Cindy Corey)
- *Groups: Process and Practice*, Tenth Edition (2018, with Marianne Schneider Corey and Cindy Corey)
- *I Never Knew I Had a Choice*, Eleventh Edition (2018, with Marianne Schneider Corey and Michelle Muratori)
- *Theory and Practice of Group Counseling*, Ninth Edition (and *Student Manual*) (2016)

- *Group Techniques,* Fourth Edition (2015, with Marianne Corey, Patrick Callanan, and J. Michael Russell)
- *Case Approach to Counseling and Psychotherapy,* Eighth Edition (2013)

Gerald Corey has also made several educational DVD programs on various aspects of counseling practice: (1) Individual counseling video to accompany *Counseling Gwen From Various Perspectives* (2021); (2) Group video to accompany *Theory and Practice of Group Counseling* (2019); (3) *Ethics in Action: DVD and Workbook* (2015, with Marianne Schneider Corey and Robert Haynes); (4) *Groups in Action: Evolution and Challenges DVD and Workbook* (2014, with Marianne Schneider Corey and Robert Haynes); (5) DVD for *Theory and Practice of Counseling and Psychotherapy: The Case of Stan and Lecturettes* (2013); (6) DVD for *Integrative Counseling: The Case of Ruth and Lecturettes* (2013, with Robert Haynes); and (7) DVD lecturettes to accompany *Theory and Practice of Group Counseling* (2012). All of these video programs are available through Cengage Learning.

Chapter 1

Creating Your Professional Path

Introduction

Choosing a career in counseling is more complex than simply deciding that you want to help others. In your graduate program interview, you may be asked, "Why do you want to become a counselor?" Your answer to this question may reveal both your motivations and how your personal needs may influence your work as a counseling professional. As you begin to create your professional path, reflect on these questions:

- What are your motivations for becoming a counselor?
- What rewards do you expect to gain from counseling others?
- What professional path do you envision for yourself?

If you understand your motivations for being in a counseling program, you will have a good chance of meeting the goals you set for yourself as a professional.

When I first decided to become a teacher, my conscious motivation was to help others. Eventually I realized that multiple motives were operating in my career choice. Initially I was not aware of what I would be getting from helping others. Later in my career, becoming a counseling psychologist and a counselor educator met my need for being able to make a difference in the lives of students, and this is a basic motivation that energizes me today.

Although you may have altruistic reasons for choosing your professional path, it is important to recognize what you are getting from helping others. Go deeper than simply saying you get satisfaction or a good feeling from helping others. Your desire to become a counselor might include the need to make an impact on others, to give back to society what you have been given, to understand yourself more fully or to resolve personal issues, to feel the appreciation associated with being needed, to study and understand what drives human behavior and behavioral change, or to develop answers to problems and find solutions that help others. Your professional endeavors should be satisfying. If some of your own needs are not met through your work, you may lose interest in what you are doing. Several needs and motivations may be operating at the same time, and your reasons for continuing on this path may evolve and strengthen throughout your career.

If you find meeting your clients' needs satisfying, you are more likely to create a rewarding career for yourself. But it is important to understand whose personal needs are being met through your work. Meeting your personal needs at the expense of your clients' needs is unethical. For example, if you push your agenda over that of your client because you need to see your client make behavioral changes, you are failing your client. If you have a strong need to be appreciated and praised, you may seek positive feedback from your client instead of focusing on your client's needs. Your professional path will be built based on many choices you make early in your career.

• • •

What suggestions do you have for students who are selecting a counseling career?

Reflect on what you would most like from your career, and follow your interests. If you let yourself dream about an ideal profession, what does your dream tell you? Be guided by what you most want in life, not by what you think other people want for you. Creating a career is a continuing decision-making process; it is not a single event. If you let yourself envision what you most want from your career, and if you work to achieve your goals, your accomplishments may exceed your wildest dreams. Mentors and supervisors can provide resources to help you make career choices and point out directions for you to consider. Reflect on this input as you decide what will work best for you. Instead of selecting *one* occupation that will last a lifetime, choose a broad field of endeavor that appeals to you, and remain open to taking action on opportunities that come your way.

What ideas can you offer students who are beginning their professional journey?

My career path has not proceeded in a straight line; it has been marked by many twists and turns. I began by learning about counseling in general, and then I narrowed my focus as I took other turns on my professional journey. I have found ways to maintain interest in the many aspects of my work, especially through teaching, writing, and making educational videos. Teaching has always been my primary area of interest, and from this general area I eventually developed specialized interests in counselor education, ethics in counseling practice, theory and practice of counseling and psychotherapy, and group work. Following my interests and doing what seemed most personally meaningful has been my best guide in charting my professional course.

Becoming the professional you aspire to be is a process that will evolve and change over time. Here are some ideas for you to consider as you actively create your personal and professional journey:

- Reflect on all that you *can* do rather than on what you cannot do.
- Listen to your inner voice, and strive to trust your intuitions.
- Do not hesitate to ask for help when you need it. You cannot do everything by yourself.
- Cultivate meaningful relationships with friends, colleagues, and family members who can offer you encouragement.
- Find at least one mentor to help guide you in creating your professional path.

- Talk with a number of professionals in the field you wish to pursue. Ask what they do, how they decided on their career, the pros and cons of what they are doing, and advice they may want to offer about entering the counseling profession.
- Participate in volunteer work as well as in employment or internships in the field you hope to pursue. Gaining direct experience can help you sample potential career pathways.
- Explore and take risks by trying different kinds of professional activities or working with different populations. You may discover new interests that had not previously occurred to you.
- Realize that who you are as a person has a key impact on the professional you are becoming.
- Invest in taking care of yourself in mind, body, and spirit. Realize that your ability to care for others is contingent upon you taking care of yourself.
- Be willing to obtain supervision and consultation, regardless of the stage of your career.
- Keep in touch with those people who are significant in your life.
- Learn more about how your own culture is an important part of you, and cultivate an interest in learning about people from cultures different from your own.
- Do your best to be genuine, and never lose yourself when putting on a professional demeanor.
- Put forth your best efforts, set high standards for yourself, and at the same time be kind to yourself and accept your limitations.
- Avoid burdening yourself with trying to be perfect and never making mistakes. Have the courage to be imperfect, and treat your mistakes as valuable lessons and opportunities for growth.
- Acquire and nurture a sense of humor. Avoid taking yourself too seriously, and laugh at your foibles.
- Consider how you can make a significant difference in the lives of others.
- Become a member of at least one professional organization, attend conferences, and consider presenting at conferences.
- Engage in self-reflection, and keep a personal journal.
- Envision what you would like your legacy to be.

As you review these ideas, which seem most helpful to you? Which suggestions would be most difficult for you to put into action? Which ideas are you willing to put into action right away?

One of my former students pursued a social work career, and I recently received an email from him telling me that he had accepted my challenge to take risks and how following this advice has been central in creating his professional journey. Here is part of what he shared with me.

> Recently an opportunity presented itself and I went for it. The Directorship for the Mental Health Department of an urban school district became available, I applied, and I got the position. The department consists of a large workforce of school-based mental health providers (mainly LCSWs and a few psychiatrists). There are moments when the weight of the job wakes me up in the middle of the night. However, there are more moments (at least right now) where I find the inspiration and drive to positively impact the social-emotional and mental well-being of all the students enrolled in this district . . . that's not even counting their parents/caregivers and staff!
>
> You have been in my thoughts recently. I hope all is well with you. I want you to know that I often think back on how you challenged me and how by leaning into those challenges I am the person that I am now. Thank you!

For a personal presentation on beginning your professional path, see *Surviving and Thriving in Your Counseling Program* (Austin & Austin, 2020).

How can providing service and giving back to others be a crucial part of my career?

Inspiring others has been a motivating force throughout my entire career. It gives me immense satisfaction to be a source of encouragement to my students, to provide support, and to nudge them into finding and following their passions. Providing service to others is not a completely altruistic endeavor; I am well aware of the personal satisfaction I derive from being in a position to make a difference in the lives of students and mentees. I appreciate my students' deep commitments to social justice work and to doing what they can to better their community and the world. Although this may seem ambitious and unrealistic, I am convinced that we can bring about change in the world through our desire to give back to others what we have been given. We each have unique talents, and putting these talents into action is a vital part of striving toward self-actualization.

Making small ripples has a cumulative impact that expands your influence. Many of you may have initially gravitated toward the counseling profession because of the profound impact teachers, counselors, and family members had on you, and now you want to pay it forward. Even as graduate students, many of you have already derived satisfaction and fulfillment from assisting people in navigating their struggles. Caring about others is certainly a worthy ideal, and it is essential to take care of yourself so you can sustain your efforts in providing service to others.

What blocks the effectiveness of new clinicians most at the beginning of their career?

One thing that gets in the way of the effectiveness of new professionals is trying too hard and expecting to be perfect in whatever they do. When beginning to see clients in a graduate program, students often focus on what technique to use, what to say next, and how they are being perceived by the client. It is difficult to be present with an individual client when your mind is distracted in this way. Work to put these thoughts aside and concentrate on listening to the person before you. Our task is to listen carefully and deeply to our clients and to let them lead the way. If we are able to even minimally enter the world of our clients, we increase our chances of being present for them. Counselors are not solely responsible for the outcomes of therapy. By enlisting our clients as collaborative partners in the therapeutic work, we can put more emphasis on what is happening for our clients in the present moment and use this as a guide to exploration in a session.

What advice do you have for those of us who want to make a career in the area of counselor education and supervision?

Without a doubt, taking the initiative to network with my peers, professors, and colleagues was a key factor in establishing my own career. I have been a member of organizations such as the American Counseling Association, the American Psychological Association, the National Organization for Human Services, the Association for Counselor Education and Supervision, and regional organizations for many years. I regularly attend these professional conferences and greatly enjoy and profit from attending and presenting programs with colleagues. Even at this late stage in my career, I am committed to being active in professional organizations, and I encourage you to join the professional organizations that most align with your interests.

If your area of interest is counselor education and supervision, I recommend attending the Association for Counselor Education and Supervision conferences and submitting proposals to present a program at their national or regional conferences. Becoming a member of the American Counseling Association and attending their annual conferences can provide you with rewarding experiences. Attending these conferences is a great way to make connections with people who share your interests in counselor education and supervision. Being active in a professional organization will help you stay current in your field, increase the scope of your network of colleagues, and discover available positions in your field. Schedule some time with your professors and ask them how you can get established in a career in academia. You do not have to carve out your professional career on your own, and reaching out to those who can mentor you is one way to learn about key opportunities.

What advice do you have for new counselor educators about successfully navigating the tenure and promotion process?

I have never been overly worried about getting tenure. In fact, I left several secure teaching positions for new positions that promised to lead to professional advancement. In my last position at California State University at Fullerton, I navigated the process that led to tenure and being promoted to full professor. I was guided by my professional interests, which involved a great deal of time and effort teaching and writing textbooks. Teaching and writing have been intertwined for me. I see writing as a forum for teaching, and I have written books for the courses I taught. My work as an educator enhanced my writing, and my writing was a productive resource for preparing for classes. I greatly enjoyed teaching and met with considerable success in this realm. I had high standards for my students, and even though my classes were demanding and challenging, my student evaluations were consistently positive.

When I was engaged in the tenure and promotion process, a number of criteria were deciding factors in achieving these academic mileposts: research and scholarly activities, teaching performance, publications in journals and books, service to the community and the university, and professional activities. Today many universities emphasize scholarly work and professional publications in refereed journals. When it came to advancement in the university, I was given credit for writing textbooks as a key part of scholarly activity. I was not unaware or unconcerned about meeting the research expectations of my department and the university, but my major efforts went toward doing what I loved and what was meaningful to me. The "publish or perish" pressure did not dictate my activities as a university professor. Fortunately, following this path led to tenure, promotion, and several prestigious awards based on professional achievements.

If you are a new counselor educator, I strongly recommend that you investigate the mission and goals of the university program to which you are applying and consider what will be required of you to gain tenure and advance in professional rank. Ask your colleagues who have successfully navigated the tenure/promotion process for suggestions on how you can navigate this process. You are not alone in this demanding process, and reaching out to others can be instrumental in attaining your goals. Some universities are known to have research-based programs that emphasize publishing articles in peer-reviewed journals more than writing textbooks or excelling in teaching. This may not fit your professional interests, and you may be very unhappy in your university position even though you become tenured and are promoted.

Reflection Questions

1. What do you expect to get personally from becoming a counselor and being of service to others?
2. What are your main motivations for wanting to become a counselor or a counselor educator? What are the rewards you expect from counseling others?
3. Can you identify one thing that might get in your way of being an effective counselor? In what ways can you challenge this obstacle?
4. What are your thoughts about the kind of counseling career you would like to create?
5. To what degree are you interested in attending and participating in professional conferences? What personal benefits do you see in becoming involved in a professional organization?

Chapter 2

Glimpses From My Career

Introduction

Turning points are easier to identify when looking back over six decades of professional practice. I hope my personal reflections on the various developments in my career will provide a few signposts as you travel your own professional path. I address topics such as advice I heard on designing a career, my family-of-origin experiences, balancing time between work and family, career opportunities taken and others missed, working professionally with my wife along with my wife's perspective on working with me, expectations and pressures associated with success, acquiring some degree of fame, retirement plans, and my hoped-for legacy. I hope sharing the lessons I have learned from my personal and professional experiences will help you recognize potential turning points on the professional path you are creating for yourself.

• • •

What was the most significant advice you received early in your career?

I received this advice early in my career, and it provided the foundation for my journey: Find your passion, and take active steps in letting this passion be your guide in developing your professional identity. I have remained open to opportunities that might change my professional path, and I have willingly lived with the uncertainty that changes in my career path might include. For the most part, I have no regrets about choosing to leave a secure position and accept a new position, even though the outcome of this choice was uncertain at the time. I valued asking friends, family members, and colleagues for their recommendations when I was wondering what career decisions to make. However, I also learned that the ultimate decision was mine. For me, taking calculated risks many times over has paid off.

I have greatly enjoyed all the phases of my career and found most aspects of my work to be rewarding; however, it was not easy for me to accept the fact that I could not do everything that I found professionally rewarding. Sometimes I accepted too many work projects and discovered the limits of my time and energy, and I learned that it is necessary to recognize my limitations. I learned that I needed to take time to reflect on the commitments I already had before taking on additional responsibilities. It was difficult to decline some attractive invitations, and I have done my best to avoid feeling guilty when I decided not to accept a request. A key message I often give to my students is to carefully consider what professional projects you can realistically accept. If you take on too many tasks and roles and cannot follow through with your commitments, you have created problems for all concerned. Many of us need to learn to say no without guilt. It is far better to realize your limitations than to promise to deliver and fail to make good on your promise.

What can you say about the influence of your family of origin that prompted you to choose a career in counseling?

I am a first-generation Italian American, and although both of my parents were from Italy, neither of them spoke Italian at home nor did they think it was important that I learn Italian. My family name was originally Cordileone, meaning "heart of the lion," but my father changed it to Corey because he thought

Italians were not valued in America at that time. When I was a child, we spent many weekends at family gatherings with my grandparents. I felt lost because my grandparents and other relatives spoke very little English so most of the conversations were in Italian. A theme of my early years was feeling ignored by my family of origin. My brother was 13 years older than I was, and another brother died when he was 6 years old, which happened before I was born. Basically I grew up as an only child. My brother and I had the same parents, yet most people would never guess we were brothers because we had very little in common. He served in World War II as a pilot in the Air Force when I was a child, and after the war he left for college to study business and had a successful business career. We were polar opposites in terms of values, perspectives on life, religious beliefs, and political views. Although we had the same parents, it seems as though we grew up in two different cultures. In spite of our differences, we had a cordial relationship and kept in contact until he died at age 83. It pleased me that he seemed proud of my accomplishments in the professional world and would talk to his golf buddies about my books. He often teased me, saying he was surprised by my success and that he felt I would never amount to anything given my track record of failure in elementary school.

My father, Joseph (Guiseppi), was a brilliant and sensitive man, but he suffered from anxiety and depression for much of his life. Sent from Italy to New York by his father when he was 7 years old, he was raised in an orphanage. Against all odds, he went to a dental college and later practiced dentistry, which was possible because his father gave him $10,000 to pursue his education and career. That was a very generous source of financial and emotional support. My father's depressive condition had a major impact on me as a child, an adolescent, and as a young adult. In addition to losing their 6-year-old son to leukemia, my parents lost all of their financial assets during the Great Depression. On the day of their son's funeral, the landlord came to issue a foreclosure notice on their house. Later my father had to quit his dental practice because of what he referred to as his "nervous breakdown." He then worked for relatives at menial jobs to provide for the family. These crises contributed to my father becoming very conservative and avoiding taking any risks. When I became a teacher during my early adulthood, my father's advice to me was to choose the safe path and not to take risks or give up a secure teaching position lest I not succeed in another position.

I am sure my father and mother were disappointed when I came home from school and sadly reported that I did not get promoted from the fifth to the sixth grade. This was a source of embarrassment to me, and I felt some shame for letting my parents down. My father helped me with my homework, especially in arithmetic, and he was less than patient with my inability to grasp simple arithmetic problems. My fear of math followed me into my doctoral program, and I almost dropped out because I was sure I could not pass the required statistics courses. My father died at the age of 70, shortly before I received my doctorate in counseling when I was 30. He never saw me achieve this academic marker, nor did he witness any of my professional accomplishments. At my father's funeral, I decided that I did not want to follow his path of choosing safety over venturing into new territory. I vowed never to let depression dominate my life, as it had done with him. Keeping busy and plunging into work activities for most of my life is one strategy I have used to keep depression at bay. Part of my motivation to attend graduate school and pursue a career in counseling may have been to make up for the lost opportunities to help my father overcome his bouts of depression. Another driving force was striving for my father's acceptance of me and doing what would make him proud of me. When I told my mother about my professional accomplishments, she would say that was terrific and that she knew my father would have been so proud!

My mother, Josephine, lived to be 94, and she was a great teacher for me by modeling her way of living. From her early childhood years, she worked hard on her father's peach orchard and learned the values of a simple life. She loved school and had a keen desire to learn, but she was not allowed to pursue education beyond high school. She several times related to me that her father had kept her out of school for a few weeks at the beginning of a school year because he needed her to work on his farm. Her father needed the help of all his children to bring produce to downtown Los Angeles every morning by horse and wagon, which meant that my mother had to put her needs on the back burner. My mother was very sad that she was unable to grasp algebra because she missed the first few weeks of school.

Despite having a hard life, my mother retained her wit and sense of humor throughout her life. She taught me the value of hard work and showed me that one can age gracefully and continue to make changes even in old age. My mother was curious and interested in people, always wanting to hear the latest gossip. Unlike my father, she was a risk taker, found ways to financially take care of the family when my father was unable to do so, and enjoyed her life and all of her friends. She was especially involved in Marianne's and my daughters' lives and greatly enjoyed time with them, as they did with her. My mother was frequently impatient with me and had no trouble letting me know this. She realized that my interests were somewhat narrow, and she challenged me in caring and humorous ways. Contrary to my father, my mother worked with me patiently on learning the multiplication tables, and she tutored me in arithmetic at my grandfather's peach orchard where we spent weekends.

I have a great deal of love and affection for both my mother and father. I did my best to show them that I cared, strove to accomplish academic goals in graduate school, and wanted their recognition and approval. My mother and father had a strained relationship, and I am sure their frustrations left a mark on me in several ways. I wonder if growing up in my family spurred my drive to become a counselor. Although I could not help them individually or as a couple, I might be able to use the lessons I learned from them to offer assistance to others. Pursuing graduate school and becoming a counselor was, in part, due to my feelings of inferiority over doing so poorly in elementary school and striving to compensate for my early failures. A lesson I learned was that failure does not have to be fatal and that I could conquer my feelings of inadequacy by succeeding later in my academic pursuits.

How did you balance your time between work and family throughout your busy career?

Marianne and I had been married for only a few years when I became a father to two daughters—a role for which I was not prepared. In all honesty, I was pretty much an absent father in their early years. I struggled through the process of learning how to be a father, and I had many things to learn about being a husband who could share family duties. I put most of my time into carving out my career, and in those days gender roles were pretty clearly defined. I made my career my primary role, and I was satisfied leaving the caretaking roles and household tasks to my wife, Marianne. I did not do a good job of balancing my work life with my family life during these early years of our marriage.

Despite my devotion to my work, there were many positive aspects to our family life. We did go on family vacations, visited Germany (Marianne's home town) for several weeks every summer, frequently went to the beach and the mountains, and went on outings with other families. As a couple, we arranged to have time alone for vacations, which was important for our relationship. This gave our young daughters time with their grandmother, which they relished. Taking this time as a family, and also as a couple, was important in helping us remain productive in our professional lives. I became a more attentive father once our children were in middle school and high school. Looking back, I do have some regrets for not having shared more of the family responsibilities and not doing a better job of monitoring my time and devotion to my professional life.

What have been some significant turning points for you in your career?

In the early 1960s, I began my professional career as a high school English teacher. Until I became a young adult, I had not thought that my existence mattered. Becoming a teacher was a turning point that contributed to feeling that my life was meaningful. Teaching was a most rewarding endeavor, and I did my best to make learning interesting and personally relevant to my students' lives. I was willing to take risks, and I experimented with novel ways of teaching in all of my classes.

My 4-year stint of teaching high school students was followed by 2 years teaching psychology in a community college. It was relatively easy to structure introductory psychology courses in a way that challenged students to engage in self-exploration and to talk about their personal concerns. My courses emphasized discussion and small-group work, which tweaked my growing interest in group counseling. As a high school teacher and community college instructor, my passion was to personalize learning by connecting the subjects I was teaching to the lives of the students. I devised many ways to get students to participate in class discussions and experiential activities. My teaching experience demonstrated that students do not personalize their learning simply by listening to lectures and taking notes; they internalize their learning by raising questions, sharing their thoughts and experiences, interacting with one another on topics that are personally significant to them, and reflecting and writing about what they experience in life and learn in the classroom.

I left my job as a community college psychology instructor, which was a secure position, to accept a position in both teaching and working at the counseling center at a 4-year university, California State Polytechnic University in Pomona (Cal Poly). When I began working with college students in the counseling center, it was difficult for me to get a sense of my effectiveness. My self-confidence began to erode, and I wondered whether I would ever become as skilled a therapist as my colleagues were. A lesson I learned from working in the counseling center was the value of persisting, even in the absence of external validation. It helped to tell myself that I probably would not be as effective at the beginning as I expected to be throughout my time doing this work.

I also taught a variety of psychology courses and eventually specialized in teaching educational psychology classes for students preparing to become elementary or secondary teachers. I held this position for 5 years, earned tenure, and was very happy teaching in the education and psychology programs at Cal Poly, but I did not assume that I had to remain in this position until retirement.

A new opportunity appeared that would mean giving up my tenured position for a different kind of program that seemed professionally exciting. The move I contemplated was certainly risky, but I had found that taking risks was rewarding. In 1972, I applied to teach at an innovative undergraduate human services program at California State University at Fullerton. Being part of an innovative student-centered program lured me away from my secure position to this new and uncertain opportunity. This was a time when I disregarded my father's advice to stay with what was safe and known. A lesson that I relearned then was that most professional moves entail a degree of risk as well as the promise of new and exciting opportunities. Over my career, I have typically been willing to choose an unknown path that entailed some risks rather than remain on a familiar safe path.

The human services program was truly unique and attracted some bright and dedicated students. The program integrated the cognitive and affective domains, and students majoring in human services found their classes both academically demanding and personally meaningful. I have had a rich career in this program since 1972, and I have never regretted accepting this position.

You've done a good deal of research and writing during your career. What gaps in research would you explore and what data would you collect if you could go back in time?

My colleagues and I have engaged in many writing projects over the years, but I have not been actively involved in doing research. If I could go back in time, I would make a greater effort to combine the roles of practitioner and researcher instead of giving my full attention to practitioner and teacher. Each year my colleagues and I facilitated two weeklong residential therapeutic groups as a part of the continuing education program. Each of these groups had four professional group facilitators and 16 group members. These groups were experiential courses for human services and counseling students. My colleagues and I missed some key opportunities for doing research on these therapeutic groups. Had we conducted research on the process and outcomes of these 50+ groups we were involved with over 25 years, we would have some additional objective data about what works in groups to supplement our subjective knowledge. Because these group courses involved academic credit (as an elective), participants were required to put together a personal reading program prior to and after the group. They also wrote several papers that entailed reflection and evaluation of their experience in the group and the impact it had on their life once they left the group. These papers revealed significant personal learning and how these insights could be transferred to daily life.

Carl Rogers did important process research with clients in both individual and group counseling. If we wanted to discover the impact of therapeutic experiences, Rogers often stated that we should ask those involved to share their subjective perspectives. The papers participants in our groups wrote did provide glimpses of their subjective experience in the group, not only during the week they were in the group but in the weeks and months following the group experience. I wish we had been systematic in collecting data from the members as soon as they enrolled in the group course, during the intensive week itself, and at different points after they left the group. I am convinced that systematic qualitative research would have shed considerable light on specific factors in the group process that resulted in personality and behavior changes.

What has it been like for you and your wife, Marianne, to work as a professional team? Are your personal and professional lives complementary?

Marianne and I have been married for 55 years, and for almost 50 years we have been actively involved in many professional endeavors as a team. We cofacilitated weeklong residential therapeutic groups for university students in a continuing education course each summer for 25 years. This was a highly rewarding experience that gave us a window into how group work can transform lives. We learned incredible lessons about the best of humanity when a group is committed to being honest with itself and others. I believe Marianne and I complement each other as group therapists. We share a similar philosophy regarding how to promote awareness and change in group members, but we each have our own unique personality and therapeutic style. I learned a great deal from Marianne about how to be present with individuals and how to facilitate therapeutic work with both individuals and the group as a whole. We are able to work together as a team without power plays or jealousies. We are often told that the way we are in the group is similar to how we are when we are not functioning in our professional roles.

We have been involved in training workshops for professionals in group work for many years and have conducted training and supervision groups in the United States and in other countries as well. Workshops in other countries provide opportunities for us to learn ways of adapting our counseling philosophy and approach to many different cultural contexts. Marianne has been my primary multicultural mentor, teaching me about culture and how to think about understanding diversity and incorporate this understanding in the practice of group counseling.

We have also teamed up for many presentations and live demonstrations at various universities for continuing education of both counseling students and professionals. These team presentations were far more impactful than if I had done them alone. Participants have opportunities to observe how our different styles are complementary. I greatly enjoy the times when we teach as a team because this enhances the liveliness and depth of the presentations.

Marianne and I have collaborated on several educational videos and have written many books together. I am frequently asked, "What is it like to write books as a couple?" I am convinced that our professional work as a team in facilitating groups, leading group training workshops, and giving presentations at professional conferences has provided the foundation for developing and refining our collective ideas about group counseling and ethics in counseling practice. Our video, *Ethics in Action*, grew out of our many discussions about bringing ethical dilemmas to life by enactment through role playing. Our group videos, *Evolution of a Group* and *Challenges Facing Group Leaders*, gave us an opportunity to demonstrate our co-leadership skills, and the unfolding of a group was brought to life from the pages of the books we coauthored. In addition, the videos provided a way to reach many more students.

In writing and revising our books, we bounce ideas off each other, which is truly an interactive process that fosters creativity. Marianne has been a source of inspiration for me for our coauthored books as well as books that I have authored alone. We each bring different strengths to our writing projects. Marianne has a talent for providing real-life examples from her clinical experiences and for making sure our writing has practical and realistic applications. Marianne is particularly adept at pruning extraneous details and ensuring that examples illustrate a key message. My strengths are bringing my teaching experiences into the writing and my ability to integrate material by conceptualizing and organizing ideas. I also have a good sense of what helps students understand the practical applications of counseling principles and theories.

Although Marianne and I share many values, at times we disagree on the importance of certain topics. I have learned that respectful disagreements or discussions of differing perspectives can be extremely valuable in teaching, in conducting groups, and in writing textbooks. We are sustained in our efforts by the generally positive feedback we receive from both students and professionals who use our books and videos. When Marianne and I function as a team, we are able to bring a higher level of excellence to our work. However, over the years I have learned that gender bias is alive and well in the counseling profession. Books that we have coauthored have far too often been credited to me as sole author. As in other professional fields, counseling professionals have some way to go in recognizing the contributions of women, especially when they team up with a man.

It can be challenging to navigate our professional work alongside our relationship apart from work. We continue to monitor how our work together enhances or detracts from a satisfactory personal relationship and rebalance our priorities when needed.

To Marianne Schneider Corey

What has it been like for you and your husband, Jerry, to work as a professional team? Are your personal and professional lives complementary?

I (Marianne) was licensed as a marriage and family therapist in 1976 and started a private practice working primarily with individuals, couples, and some families. I enjoyed my work and was certainly not looking for a different type of work. However, I had underestimated Jerry's powers of persuasion. Anyone who knows Jerry will attest to how challenging it is to say no to him. The first time I said no to him was when he proposed to me. I was on my way to Germany after a year and a half stay in the United States. At that time, I had no intention of living in the United States permanently. I eventually did return to America, we married, and we have been married for 55 years. We came from very different worlds, which I think has influenced our work as a team. We had to come to terms with many differences. I grew up in Germany under Hitler's reign during World War II and was raised on a farm in a small village in Germany. Jerry was an Italian American raised in Beverly Hills, California. The most challenging hurdle was that he was Catholic and I was Protestant. Also, I wanted to live in Germany, and he wanted to live in the United States. We had many heated discussions, which sometimes turned into arguments, before we were married. Jerry's mother often said, "The two of you will never make it!" In spite of her prediction and our differences, we continue our journey.

When Jerry invited me to cofacilitate some of the groups he was leading, I agreed without realizing I was beginning a journey that has continued for more than 50 years. I also had no intention of writing books, and that changed largely due to Jerry's persuasive talents and infectious excitement for a project. Both of us were passionate about our work as group facilitators, and we witnessed the impact of group work on the lives of participants in our workshops and groups. We also had witnessed some of the abuses of group work during the 1960s and 1970s. Our many discussions about how group therapists could avoid the common ethical pitfalls we had seen led us to write our first group counseling textbook, which was published in 1977. All of our books grew out of our interest and experience in the topics we wrote about and were based on our teaching and practice. We knew the students we were writing for, and we wanted to inspire them with our excitement about the subject.

Our initial differences as a couple became a real asset in our professional work together. We learned how to disagree, which we do often, yet we realized that our basic philosophy for the counseling profession was very much aligned. We learned never to ignore our differences but to respect them and to recognize our strengths. We both see it as important to attend to our personal relationship and to be aware of how it may affect our professional work as a team. I am convinced that our ability to work together for so many years is because we make time for our personal life. We have our individual interests and life, and we have a life as a couple. We are honest with each other and recognize when our work is interfering with our personal life, and we make the necessary changes. We have cultivated wonderful friends and colleagues who have been a great support to both of us during times of personal and professional difficulties. Any one of our friends and colleagues would most likely tell you that Marianne and Jerry disagree a lot, but somehow they seem to work things out.

We do banter and tease each other often when we copresent at professional workshops. Our audiences seem to enjoy our sense of humor and our way of being with each other and presenting in a practical and personal way. We are not competitive, and we have a clear sense of ourselves. We are aware of how we can make a difference, both individually and as a couple. I have cultivated a strong ego, which has made it possible for us to work together for a lifetime.

As a couple, we had to avoid the pitfalls of believing the adulation from some of our group members. Group members sometimes perceive us as the "ideal couple." It has been important for both of us to recognize that they may have a need to see us as being ideal, but we cannot afford to be flattered by their adulation. As members get to know us, we think they begin to see us more realistically. If we believed their perceptions, we might have ignored certain realities when life was not so perfect and stopped working on ourselves individually and on our relationship.

It has been and continues to be a challenge for me not to allow the frequent insensitive gender-biased reactions to me to have a negative effect on my personal and professional life. Too often our combined coauthored books are referred to as Gerald Corey's books. Gender bias is a present-day reality, even among some female colleagues who argue for gender equality and for giving professional women the credit they deserve. I think it is especially problematic for professional colleagues who are also in an intimate relationship. I avoid reacting defensively and recognize that these attitudes are slow to change—but they are changing.

We continue to enjoy attending professional conferences such as the American Counseling Association, the Association for Counselor Education and Supervision, the American Psychological Association, the American Group Psychotherapy Association, and the National Organization for Human Services. It is rewarding to both of us when people acknowledge the impact our work has had on them. We especially admire the enthusiasm, devotion, and social justice dedication to the counseling profession that younger colleagues manifest at these conferences. We frequently comment that our profession is in good hands going forward.

• • •

Looking back over your career, Jerry, do you wish you had done some things differently?

At the beginning of my career, I did not feel very competent or creative. In truth, it is probable that I was not very helpful when I first began working with clients. I was too preoccupied with how I was doing and what my clients thought of me to allow myself to be an effective counselor. If I could replay some of my first experiences as a counselor, I would be more active in my supervision and talk more about my insecurities, my self-doubts, and my inordinate need for positive feedback from clients. I would be more open with my supervisor in discussing my relationship to my clients, especially questioning how what I was doing (or not doing) was influencing our work together. When I first began as a counselor practitioner, I did not realize how critical it is to engage in honest self-reflection. It was only later that I saw how my personal problems got in the way of my clinical effectiveness. We all begin our counseling career at a single point in time, and we are likely to become more confident and effective in our work as we gain clinical experience if we are open to feedback from our clients, our supervisors, and our colleagues.

In the beginning, I did not realize the depth of commitment that is required to grow from a neophyte into an experienced practitioner. However, if I could replay the progression of my career, I cannot think of anything I would do differently. I consistently took the road less traveled, and doing so led to success in my profession. Eventually I realized that being guided by my interests and being open to new vistas kept me engaged and vital.

At any point in your career, did you feel pressure that you could not meet what was expected of you as you became more successful?

I feel pressure to keep my professional commitments, pressure to maintain a realistic work schedule, and pressure to meet a multitude of requirements. Most of the pressure I have experienced did not come from others; it was self-imposed and based on demands I made on myself. Experiencing success did not seem to create additional pressures on my ability to perform. Perhaps this is because I knew what I expected of myself as a professor and as a writer. I did my best to live up to my own expectations rather than attempting to live by what others expected of me. I strive to do my best in all my professional endeavors, and I am helped by knowing that I do not need to reach for perfection; there is room for being imperfect. I learned to tell myself that pressure is not necessarily bad or something to be avoided at all costs. It is how I interpret pressure, what it does to me, and how I manage it that counts.

How does fame affect your relationship with colleagues and peers in the counseling field?

Honestly, I have not seen myself as being famous, nor have I directly worked to achieve fame in my professional life. I have tried to follow my heart and to do what I found to be meaningful. I have done my best to contribute to the betterment of my students and to the counseling profession. I have included my peers, colleagues, and students in many of my projects, and I do my best to remember that any successes I enjoy are the result of a team effort. I am not driven by competition, and whatever fame I may have acquired has not affected my collegial relationships. Being mindful of my support from colleagues and my good fortune in having been afforded so many rich opportunities goes a long way toward keeping me humble.

I am often pleasantly surprised when I attend professional conferences and find so many people at the presentations my colleagues and I give. I am equally surprised at how many graduate students stand in line during a book signing event at a conference to get their book signed, to take a photo, and to chat briefly. Sometimes students request a selfie with me, and I admit that I do enjoy these interactions and this attention. When students and professors tell me how the books my colleagues and I have written are special to them, I appreciate their acknowledgment, and it motivates me to continue contributing to the field.

Being in the spotlight does have one drawback. When I leave a conference and am on the street walking, nobody stops me to ask for a photo! I go through attention withdrawal each time a conference ends.

Do you have any plans for retirement? What holds your interest in the counseling profession today?

I formally retired from the university system as a full-time professor in 2000 at age 63. However, I have continued to teach several courses each year. I have also continued writing and revising books, making educational videos, and attending and presenting at professional conferences. At age 72 in 2010, in *Creating My Professional Path*, I wrote that I greatly enjoyed all the various facets of my work life and did not see retirement as part of my future picture. Interacting with colleagues on exciting projects was meaningful and enjoyable, and I found joy in working with appreciative and eager students who kept me young. Today, at age 82, I am able to say basically the same thing I said 10 years ago. What keeps my interest in being actively engaged in the counseling field is believing that I still have more to contribute, especially to graduate students and new professionals. I love teaching and find it energizing. I greatly enjoy my students and appreciate keeping in contact with my colleagues. Teaching also keeps me up to date in the counseling profession. Writing textbooks and making educational videos enable me to reach students beyond my own classroom. I am grateful for my excellent health and my good life, which allows me to continue in my pursuit of meaningful professional goals. Much of what I have achieved professionally over the past 58 years is the result of working professionally with Marianne and with our many colleagues and friends in the profession. Our work together and our discussions continue to be the impetus for new ideas and new projects, and I expect these collaborations to continue in the years ahead. I have no plans yet to retire, but slowing the pace down over the past decade was, and still is, a good strategy.

As I was writing about my reluctance to retire, I received an email from an undergraduate human services student who recently applied for a social work master's program and was accepted. He was a very active and involved student in my group counseling class last semester. Here is how Jeremy Rintalan challenged himself and found his own path toward a professional counseling career:

> I want to take a moment and let you know that I was accepted into graduate school. I will be studying at the Department of Social Work and was granted a scholarship. My fieldwork placement for this upcoming school year will be working with children and families. At times, I find myself in disbelief that my life has taken a turn for the best. And with that, it has not been easy overcoming these irrational thoughts that I do not deserve to be where I am now in my personal, professional, and academic life. But here I am, making the best of what I have, and I am so thankful for my family, for my education, and for all the support I have received. With that being said, I wanted to take a moment and just say thank you for everything you have done, not only for me as my professor, but for all the lives you have impacted. You have impacted my life. You are truly a remarkable individual, an inspirational leader, and someone I will hold near to my head and heart for the rest of my life. Even now working as a drug and alcohol counselor, I hear you talking about Albert Ellis and how he would say we have to push ourselves (PYA, or Push Your Ass) if we want change. I tell this to my clients all the time! One day I hope to have an opportunity that will allow me to give back all that I have been fortunate enough to receive while in your class and as a human services student.

Jeremy is exceeding his dreams and is engaged in becoming a competent social worker. It is students like him that motivate me to continue teaching and that make it very difficult for me to imagine retiring.

What would you want your legacy to be?

In March 2014, I was the recipient of a Living Legends Award at an American Counseling Association conference, which was a true honor. I must admit I appreciate receiving this award while still alive rather than being a dead legend. Awards have some merit, but they are only symbolic to me. The legacy that I hope will live on is being remembered by the many students who have crossed my path and that they have been inspired to use their gifts to make a difference in the lives of many others. I hope the students and professionals that I have been privileged to teach have found their voice and are using it. It is of the utmost importance to me to challenge and encourage students to identify their passion and life's mission and to take actions to bring out the goodness in others as they continue to do in themselves.

Jim Bitter, a colleague and friend, recently sent an email congratulating me on a new book. His thoughts were deeply touching and spoke to the difference we each can make that is so dear to my legacy-to-be.

> It is an honor to know you, to be friends with you, to learn from you, to feel a bond to you, both personally and professionally, as the best that humanity has to offer. When I get discouraged living in this world, I remember that you are also in this world, making a difference that is a real difference, a difference that matters, and we are friends. I feel blessed.

In short, I hope the difference I have made in the lives of others will continue to make a difference even when I am no longer on this planet.

Reflection Questions

1. As you read my personal reflections, what most stands out for you? Are there any ways you can apply my reflections to your life?
2. How has your family of origin influenced your professional ambitions and goals? Do you think your childhood experiences influenced your choice to enter the counseling profession?
3. Who in your life can be a source of inspiration and guidance for you in making decisions about your career path?
4. If you ask your mentor for advice about your career, what kind of advice would you be seeking?
5. If you were to create your legacy, what would you want it to be?

Chapter 3

Mentoring Students

Introduction

Students often ask, "How can I find a mentor?" Potential mentors may be found among your friends, fellow students, family members, counselors, professors, supervisors, and sometimes in surprising places. Some will offer guidance and suggestions, others may support your efforts as you navigate through your educational and professional career. Your personal and professional journey may take you down different paths along the way, and mentors can be extremely useful and supportive. Be clear in your own mind about how this person could be most useful to you. If you feel reluctant to approach a potential mentor, I encourage you to challenge your fears and reach out to those who could be most helpful to you. Ask whether this person has the time and interest to take on another mentee, and you may be surprised at the answer. Mentoring is a reciprocal relationship, so think about what you have to offer as well as what you hope to gain from this relationship. Perhaps collaborating and working with this person will benefit both of you. Before you approach a potential mentor, ask yourself, "What do I want to learn from this mentoring experience?"

• • •

What are some suggestions for making mentoring a meaningful experience?

Mentors can have a powerful influence in helping us achieve our personal and professional goals. Whenever I felt discouraged during my graduate school experience and early in my career, having people who believed in me gave me a sense of hope. I recognize now how much I valued the belief my mentors had in me, especially when my self-doubts could easily have gotten the best of me.

In my mentoring relationships, I try to teach those I mentor to think for themselves and to speak for themselves. I want to empower them so they can create the kind of professional life they have envisioned. Here are some thoughts I share with my mentees about how to get the most from a mentoring experience:

- Find your own passions and dreams rather than following another's design for you.
- A mentor may help you find your passion, but you have to take action to pursue your passion.
- As you learn important lessons from your mentors and faculty, put these lessons through your own filter to personalize them.
- If you idealize your mentor, do so for only a short time.
- Experiment and create your own unique style of helping that fits you; stop yourself from attempting to imitate your mentors' styles.
- Reflect on interpersonal qualities modeled by your mentors, such as demonstrating empathy, compassion, understanding, humility, authenticity, and the ability to create a trusting relationship. Strive to acquire these qualities in yourself.
- Find a group of supportive people to offer you encouragement when you are troubled with self-doubt or feel discouraged, but seek people who are willing to challenge you.
- Mentoring is a venture that can benefit both the mentee and the mentor. Realize that you also have something to offer to your mentors.
- Regardless of where you are on your academic or career path, look for ways to teach others what you have learned. Finds ways to give back to others what you have received.
- Think about the kind of mentoring you want for yourself and the kind of mentor you want to be to others.

- Mentoring is a multifaceted relationship encompassing career, personal life, and key life transitions such as beginning your career. Choose mentors who can support your development through these life transitions.
- Reflect on ways you can build on what you have learned from mentors to develop a better relationship with yourself and also with others.

A highly informative book for learning more about mentoring is *The Elements of Mentoring* (Johnson & Ridley, 2018).

What teachers and mentors influenced you most? What are some lessons you learned from your mentors?

Teachers who both challenged me and offered me support and guidance when I did not have faith in my own abilities are the most memorable for me. There were times when I doubted that I was cut out for a doctoral program in counseling or that I had what it took to be an effective counselor. The mentorship of certain professors stopped me from giving up and gave me the courage to persist and to pursue my goals. In my doctoral program, several classes in statistics were required. I was terrified and felt like dropping out of the program due to my math anxiety. My major professor assured me that my goals were attainable if I was willing to work hard and to persist. It is easy to feel engulfed by fear and to stop too soon. I learned from my professor that obstacles are stepping stones that I could use to overcome my fears. By sharing my fears with trusted others, I was able to take control of them, and they became manageable. With the help of a tutor, I passed statistics with a B, which delighted me. This experience taught me that I needed to acquire the discipline to apply myself to learning difficult subjects, to never quit, and to ask for help.

My best teachers and mentors did more than pass on information. They motivated me to want to learn and to believe that I had some gifts to share. When I saw no light, they helped me find my way. They had more faith in me than I had in myself, and that was an inspiration to me.

How have your experiences with mentors influenced your way of mentoring students?

Students often do not have confidence in voicing their beliefs, or they believe that others will not listen to them. I nudge these students to begin to act as if they could articulate their thoughts and present them in a compelling way. It is rewarding to me to see these students begin to take the risk of speaking. In my mentoring relationships, I try to do more than advocate *for* mentees. I want those I mentor to arrive at their own conclusions; I do not want a group of disciples. My hope is that they will accept challenges, take risks, pursue their passions, believe that they can make a difference, and come to understand that their unique talents can make the world a better place. I assure my students and mentees that they each have unique gifts and that they can facilitate change in individuals, groups, and society if they are willing to use their gifts.

Recently, I received this email from a student I taught in the early 1990s:

> I just want to say thank you for being my mentor during my time in the Human Services program. Your guidance, teachings, and kindness have always stuck with me and helped in my own personal and professional growth over the years.

Another student I had in recent years let me know how my mentoring has inspired her:

> I feel lucky to have had the opportunity to take two classes with you. You have inspired me to believe in myself and to always strive for more.

These messages tell me that my efforts in mentoring are indeed worthwhile, and this motivates me to continue doing what I can to mentor students. Hearing that I was instrumental in their personal and professional development is gratifying, and I continue to enjoy giving students encouragement, believing in them, and providing some inspiration as they learn to give credit to themselves for becoming the person and counselor they choose to be.

One of the undergraduate courses I teach is for students who want to gain knowledge, skills, and supervised experience both as a member and as a facilitator of a group. I generally coteach this course with a former student who has a master's degree in counseling and is a licensed counselor. Other former students volunteer to be guest speakers and offer valuable practical information about succeeding in graduate school and creating a professional path. Students also participate as group members and take turns coleading with other members in their group two or three times during the semester, with supervision from graduate students that I supervise. These graduate students consistently tell me how much they learn by supervising these small groups and providing feedback in the group. The students in these groups greatly value the supervision they get from students who were in the group course they are now taking. I mentored many of these graduate students, and they are now peer mentors for my undergraduate students.

Almost all my students in this course aspire to pursue graduate studies in either counseling or social work. Many of them are first-generation students who are willing to challenge themselves both academically and personally. They may lack confidence in their abilities at the beginning of the course, but most of them make significant gains and come to believe that they can achieve their dreams.

I also meet with students outside of class who want to prepare themselves for applying to a graduate program. As an indirect way of mentoring, I invite faculty from counseling and social work programs to talk to my class about their respective programs. The graduate students who supervise the small groups also make themselves available to answer questions my students have about graduate programs. I think this course truly provides mentorship experiences for the students that goes well beyond learning about counseling theories and acquiring skills in group facilitation.

During my entire career, I have been motivated by a desire to make a difference. I receive the most satisfaction from helping students chart their personal and professional journey. Getting my students to challenge themselves by questioning life and encouraging them to pursue their dreams has always been more significant to me than merely presenting academic knowledge. My work does not end with me but continues through my students as they accomplish goals they did not dream were possible.

Reflection Questions

1. Throughout your education, what teachers and mentors made the most impact on you? In what specific ways?
2. What kind of person would you hope to choose as a mentor?
3. What kind of experience would you ideally want in a mentoring relationship?

4. In navigating through your educational and professional career, who are some people you could ask to be a mentor for you?

5. What are a few ways you could be helpful to a mentor? How could mentoring be beneficial to both you and your mentor?

Chapter 4

Graduate School and Beyond

Introduction

A variety of personal and academic demands are made of students in their graduate program. If you are like many graduate students, you may wonder if you deserve to be in graduate school, and this self-doubt may extend into your early career. When I was a novice counselor, I wrestled with the challenge of believing that I had something of value to offer those seeking professional assistance. It took some time for me to begin to believe that I might someday get better at the craft of counseling. It is natural to wonder if you have what it takes to make a difference in the lives of your clients. This is especially true when you first begin seeing clients professionally and have no track record to judge the effectiveness of your interventions. Trust yourself and be patient. Don't let your doubts stop you, and remain open to any feedback that provides a sense of the impact you are having on clients. As you gain experience, it becomes easier to judge your effectiveness, and former clients may let you know about the long-term value of their work with you. The questions in this chapter address a variety of concerns often raised by students in graduate school and beyond.

• • •

I am an undergraduate human services student. I want to go to graduate school but am uncertain whether to pursue a master's degree in social work or in counseling. Can you help me decide which educational route to choose?

Students considering a graduate program frequently ask whether they should apply for a social work program or a counseling program. This is a personal choice, and you need to consider your interests and career goals. Are you interested in working with communities, in securing grants, or in influencing public policy? If so, social work may be a more appropriate program. Are you primarily interested in providing individual and group counseling, working with couples and families, and doing direct clinical work? If so, a counseling program will give you the tools you need for your career. I encourage students who are undecided to visit both the counseling and the social work departments at a university they would like to attend and obtain literature on these graduate programs. It can be helpful to read the descriptions for specific required classes for each of the degrees. Do you feel excited about the classes, or are they just a means for attaining a degree? Graduate school is a major commitment; it can enrich not only your career but also your personal life. So allow your heart to become involved in the selection process.

Make an appointment with a faculty advisor in the program you are considering to learn more about the program's coursework, internship experiences, and career possibilities after obtaining a degree. Faculty are an obvious resource, but I also suggest seeking out graduate students currently enrolled in the program to gain their perspective. These students can share their experience in the program, answer questions, and provide practical tips on navigating through the program. I tell students that no decisions need to be final. You can change your area of concentration within a program even if moving to another graduate program is not realistic. Students have told me that taking these steps helped them make an informed decision about which academic route to pursue.

What should a student who is interested in the counseling profession know before beginning a graduate program?

Before entering a counseling program, students are entitled to be fully informed about what will be expected of them in the program. Just as informed consent is essential in the therapy endeavor, so too is it of paramount importance in graduate counseling programs. The language in the informed consent document must not be ambiguous, and the criteria for successful completion of the program should be easily understood by candidates. During an orientation session or at the interview with faculty, be willing to ask any questions that will help you understand what you can expect from the program as well as what is expected of you.

Graduate students often comment that their personal life was affected as they became more engaged in their studies. Some reported that their intimate relationships were disrupted and led to a parting of ways with their partner. You are likely to experience some shifts in your attitudes and changes in your behavior. Your partner may support the changes you are making or may not appreciate your changing viewpoint. One of my students said that his relationships with his mother and his brother were damaged due to value differences that arose and ways his behavior changed as he learned to broaden his view as a result of his studies.

If you involve yourself fully in a graduate counseling program, you will learn a great deal academically. You will also acquire counseling skills. And you will be expected to take an honest look at who you are and the person you want to become. A good program does far more than impart knowledge and skills basic to the counseling process. Effective training programs are designed to enable students to acquire a more complete understanding of themselves as well as gain theoretical knowledge and develop clinical skills. In a supportive and demanding environment, students are asked to evaluate their attitudes and beliefs, reflect on how their family-of-origin experiences are affecting them today, encouraged to build on their life experiences and personal strengths, and provided with opportunities to expand their awareness of self and others.

Students are expected to engage in ongoing self-reflection. Examining who you are as a person will be crucial in determining your success as a counselor, and being open to new experiences is of the utmost importance. In most training programs, students are expected to engage in appropriate self-disclosure and to participate in various personal growth activities and other forms of experiential learning. If you are not fond of letting your peers know you, counseling may not be the right program for you. Your commitment to the program will play a key role in your development as a professional counselor.

How can students get the most from graduate school, for both personal and professional development?

Having taught students in graduate school for many years, let me share some of the suggestions I have made for getting the most from your graduate program, both personally and academically. I ask my students to find ways to personally apply the content of each course. For example, when I teach a course in theories of counseling, I ask students to reflect on how they can apply key concepts of each theory to better understand their own life. When studying Adlerian therapy, I invite students to think about how their experiences in their family of origin continue to influence their present-day life. I ask them to reflect on their relationships with their parents and siblings as they were growing up. How have those relationships influenced their style of life? I expect students to master the material in the course, but I also emphasize how the course content can be applied to their personal life.

I frequently tell my students that what they are learning and practicing in their program will have a significant impact on their ability to deliver effective counseling services to others. My frequent refrain is, "Don't be satisfied with doing the minimum; put your entire self and full effort into all aspects of the program." I encourage students to get to know each other and to value the resource and support system they create for each other in meeting the personal and academic demands of the program. I suggest that students take the initiative and meet their professors during their office hours. I also list the benefits of doing volunteer work as a way to gain experience they can use currently and later in their career. My students probably tire of hearing me suggest that they attend professional conferences where they can meet students and professors from other regions. However, many students report that reaching out to people at conferences has been extremely beneficial for them.

Once I obtain a master's degree, I wonder about the advantages of pursuing a doctoral degree. Will having a doctorate offset the emotional, personal, and financial costs involved?

As soon as I received my master's degree and teaching credential at age 24, I began my career as a high school teacher. At the same time, I enrolled as a part-time student in the counselor education doctoral program at the University of Southern California. I didn't give much thought to which university to attend because this was the closest commute from where I was teaching, and taking evening classes fit nicely into my plan. I earned my EdD (Doctor of Education) degree when I turned 30. I pursued doctoral studies in counseling because I enjoyed most of my courses and thought someday I might want to teach on a university level. One of my mentors really encouraged my involvement in a doctoral program, and his trust in me was a motivational force when I made this decision. I was able to take graduate courses while being employed full-time as a high school teacher. Life was much less complicated in 1962 than it is today, and graduate studies was less of a financial burden. I remember thinking that $27 a unit was a big expense! Obtaining a doctorate opened several career options for me: becoming a licensed psychologist, beginning as a textbook author, and teaching at a university. I have never regretted the effort and time I devoted to earning a doctoral degree, and over the years I have encouraged many of my students to consider a doctoral program.

When my daughter Cindy completed two graduate degrees in counseling, I tried to persuade her to pursue a doctoral program in counseling or psychology. But she wanted to take a break from the demands of academic life and think about her own career path. With guidance and encouragement from her mentors, she eventually enrolled in a doctoral program in clinical and community psychology and graduated with a PsyD (Doctor of Psychology) degree in clinical and community psychology and later became a licensed psychologist. If you, like Cindy, need a break after earning your master's degree, spend some time reflecting on what you want in the future. Is this your choice, or is it someone else's choice for you? There are rewards and a sense of self-satisfaction in completing a doctoral degree, but you will face challenges that entail a considerable degree of sacrifice, commitment, and courage.

Students who have decided to begin a doctoral program still struggle with many questions. Which doctoral program is right for me? What steps do I need to take in being considered as a candidate? What program will best fit my interests and long-range career goals? How can I learn more about a program? Is it essential for me to have a doctoral degree to succeed in my chosen career path?

I tell interested students to thoroughly research the programs that interest them, talking with faculty, current students, and successful career counselors who followed that path. You will need to decide not only on the university but also on the specific track you want to follow for your degree. If you are interested in research activity or university teaching, a PhD program in clinical psychology or counseling psychology may suit you. If you are primarily interested in becoming a practitioner, then a PsyD may be a route to consider. If you are mainly interested in teaching in a university in a counseling program, then a PhD or EdD in counselor education might be a track to consider. The effort you put forth in gathering this information will pay rich dividends in choosing the program that best fits your interests. Certainly, a doctor's degree opens careers options that would not be possible with a master's degree, but carefully assess both costs and benefits when making this decision.

If you are considering pursuing a doctoral program, a practical guide with a wealth of information is available in a chapter titled "Getting a Doctoral Degree" in *Surviving and Thriving in Your Counseling Program* (Austin & Austin, 2020).

How did you calm your anxiety before your first session as a counselor?

It is natural to have concerns and feel unsettled on your first day of any new job. Accept the fact that you are likely to experience some anxiety as you put what you learned in graduate school into action in this new profession. You may wonder if you have what it takes to enter the world of another person. As you gain experience, you will become more confident in applying your counseling skills.

When I first began my work as a counselor, I recall feeling lost much of the time. I did not know what to say that would be helpful, and I was sure my clients saw me as inexperienced. I was anxious because I was uncertain about how to function as a counselor. I began to learn how to manage my anxiety even if I could not eliminate it. A good way to explore your anxiety is to use your journal to write down what you are thinking and feeling before you see a client or shortly after a session. Of course, talking about your anxiety with your supervisor and your fellow students can help you realize that you can control your anxiety. Before a counseling session, spend a few moments centering yourself to reduce your anxiety. Centering can be achieved just through focusing on your breathing or by engaging in mindfulness techniques. Practice techniques and exercises that you think might be useful for your clients. Take your focus away from anxiety by imagining you are with another person and are open to listening and deeply understanding this person.

As a new counselor, how can I take good notes while still being fully present with a client?

Counselors have different ways of taking notes on sessions with their clients. Some take a few key notes during the session, and this works for them and their clients. My preference is to avoid taking notes when I am with clients because it takes a good deal of attention to be fully present, to listen to what clients are saying and feeling, and to respond with empathy and caring. I certainly recommend writing case notes, even brief ones, at the end of a session with each client, if possible. Some counselors make it a practice to write case notes at the end of the day, but others say their memory is not good enough to wait for the end of the day. Talk with your clients about your ethical and legal obligation to keep adequate notes, which can be part of the informed consent process. Let them know the purpose of keeping progress notes and maintaining a current clinical record on all therapy clients.

To explore the legal aspects of keeping notes and client records, I recommend *The Counselor and the Law: A Guide to Legal and Ethical Practice* (Wheeler & Bertram, 2019).

What is your advice to new counselors who experience the imposter syndrome?

Even after earning a graduate degree or successfully obtaining a professional license, some of you might say this to yourself: "I really fooled my professors and those who thought I was deserving of a licensed. Sure, I got through all the requirements necessary to get my degree, but I am often surprised that I was able to obtain a license to practice. Although others tend to see me as being accomplished, sometimes I am convinced that I don't know what I am doing and that I do not deserve my degree or professional license."

Underneath the shadow of this imposter lie self-critical beliefs that need to be uprooted and replaced with more constructive beliefs. This sense of basic inadequacy will not vanish quickly nor completely. Even after being in the counseling profession for some time, I admit to the occasional fear of "being discovered." When giving a lecture before a large audience, I sometimes become aware of thinking: "What if I disappoint everyone here? Some might say that I can write good books, but when it comes to presenting and demonstrating counseling skills, I have a lot to learn."

If you have been concerned about being discovered, it is time to critically evaluate this negative self-talk. When you become aware of self-talk that denigrates all that you are doing professionally, apply cognitive behavioral methods to bring about cognitive restructuring. Ask yourself, "Where is the evidence that I am an imposter?" We do not have to surrender to negative beliefs that immobilize us. I have suggested to students and to clients that they act "*as if*" they are fully competent, ignoring the shadowy imposter that follows them. With a good deal of practice, feeling like an imposter can be transformed into taking pride in your professional abilities and accomplishments. Positive self-talk will shrink the size of your imposter's shadow.

What advice do you have for graduate students and those early in their careers who are trying to balance beginning a family and getting established in a career?

Attending to my personal and professional life has always been a balancing act for me. If you are early in your career and beginning a family, have many discussions with your partner about what you want as individuals and as a couple in addition to your professional aspirations. If both you and your partner are involved in professional careers, I hope you will talk about ways to share responsibilities in the home and how you can be a support system to each other in your careers. Negotiating and collaborating on how you can best work as a team can help to achieve this balance. Striving for work-life balance is an evolving process that changes over time. A former student of mine, who is now in graduate school, considers one of his major challenges to be balancing being a father with the demands of his academic career. Being at the university, holding down a job, and other family obligations make it difficult to be the father he would like to be. Even when he is physically present with his children, he is often aware of all the homework that awaits him. He has made a commitment to set time aside to be with his children and realizes that doing so offsets his self-talk that he is an uncaring and uninvolved father.

How can I find balance in my personal and professional life?

The answer to this question hinges on what kind of balance you want and in what areas you are seeking balance. If your priority is succeeding in your professional career, your time may be largely spent on work projects. If you want to have a personal life apart from your work, it is important to cultivate relationships and activities apart from work. To determine the kind of balance you hope to achieve, ask yourself this question: Do I want to *work to live*, or do I want to *live to work*?

Maintaining a balance between your personal and professional life can be a major struggle. Ideally, you will be able to invest considerable energy in your work and also to be present and connected in your home life. However, it is *not* always possible to have an ideal balance. Pressing family concerns or other urgent personal situations may command more of your attention, and at other times, the demands of your work may consume most of your energy. You may feel pressure to spend more time at your profession to keep your job or to earn a promotion. Realize that the balance between work and life will swing back and forth, and make deliberate choices to deal with this temporary imbalance.

In my own career, I have found it useful to consider the cost-benefit ratio involved in deciding how to spend my time. I have received benefits from focusing on my professional life at certain times, but definite costs were associated with my choices. At different stages in my career, I have reevaluated my values in determining what an ideal balance looks like rather than assuming that my work-life balance is a static entity. When I was in my 40s, I had considerable difficulty achieving a healthy balance between my work life and my personal life. During the academic year, I was teaching full-time and chairing the undergraduate human services program. During summers and semester breaks, I was busy writing and revising books, conducting workshops in various states, facilitating personal growth groups, and training students and professionals in group counseling. I had to learn to balance a multiplicity of professional roles, establish long-range and short-term goals, and learn how to create some personal life amidst the hectic pace of my professional life. I was greatly enjoying what I was doing professionally, yet I needed to accept that I had limitations and that I needed to find a better balance with my personal life. I eventually realized that I often took on too much because I had difficulty saying no. I began to carefully reflect on the pros and cons of accepting invitations, no matter how enticing they appeared to be.

When you consider a healthy balance between your personal and professional life, reflect on the many roles you play. Describe what an optimal work-life balance would look like for you and consider how your personal values might influence this balance. Engage in ongoing self-reflection, and assess the degree to which there is congruence between your values and your priorities.

For further reading on the topic of work-life balance, see *Counselor Self-Care* (Corey, Muratori, Austin, & Austin, 2018).

What advice about retirement do you have for those of us still in graduate school or just beginning our counseling careers?

It may seem premature to think about retirement when you are just beginning your career, but it is a good idea to project yourself into the future and imagine what you would want to say in years ahead as your career develops. What do you hope to accomplish before you reach retirement age? I have found it most useful to have both short- and long-range goals. I did not plan my professional path too far into the future, however, because I wanted to take advantage of opportunities that might come my way. When I began my teaching career in 1961, I would never have imagined that I would become a counselor educator, an author of many textbooks, and a presenter of workshops both nationally and internationally. Many of my professional goals far exceeded any of my earlier expectations. I was able to focus on my goals yet be willing to modify those goals as opportunities arose.

Many of my colleagues who have retired from their full-time positions have continued to work part-time. Some who worked in community agencies retired from that position and created a part-time private practice in counseling. Some derive satisfaction from doing volunteer work or sharing their talents in other ways. Others are fully enjoying retirement, pursuing their hobbies, spending time with family and friends, relishing in their unscheduled time, and valuing their time without the demands and stresses of work. When I ask my retired colleagues if they miss their work, most tell me they don't miss the work itself but do miss the contact with their colleagues, clients, and students. Retirement is an opportunity to redesign your life, to tap unused potentials, and to be open to a new direction that your career might take. Retirement signals a new beginning and a revitalized sense of meaning. Your task will be to discover the kind of new beginning you want to create.

Reflection Questions

1. Before being accepted in a graduate program, what did you want to know about the program and the process involved? How adequately were you informed about the expectations of the program when you applied?
2. What are you willing to do to derive the maximum benefit from your graduate program, both personally and academically?
3. In what ways, if any, can you relate to the imposter syndrome?
4. What are some of your concerns as you strive to balance your personal life with your professional life?
5. Projecting yourself into the future, what kind of retirement do you imagine you would like? What preparations can you make for a meaningful retirement at this time in your life?

Chapter 5

The Counseling Profession

Introduction

I have often been asked to comment on changes I have noticed since I began my professional career, on what I see as the major challenges of the counseling profession, on trends in the profession, and on predictions I would venture to make about the future of the counseling profession. This section deals with these topics. I encourage you to think about how you would answer each of the questions raised.

• • •

What changes have you seen in the profession from the time you started until now?

During my early career, very little attention was given to the importance of counselors learning how cultural differences influence the counseling process. We were taught counseling skills that would presumably apply to a range of clients. Today there is considerable concern over providing effective services for diverse client populations and incorporating a multicultural perspective in counseling. Multicultural counseling has moved from the background to the foreground. In addition, counselors are assuming an advocacy role in addressing social justice issues. I do not remember hearing much about counseling from a social justice perspective in the 1960s.

Relatively little attention was paid to ethical practices in counseling early in my career. Managing boundaries was not discussed, and there were many abuses by therapists who saw no need for boundaries. Today safeguards protect consumers of psychological services from unethical practitioners. During the 1960s and 1970s, sexual misconduct on the part of therapists was more common than we might think, and some therapists did not view it as a serious ethical violation. Most of the ethics codes did not specifically state that sexual activity between therapists and their clients was unethical. No ethical standards explicitly prohibited sexual relationships between counselor educators and students, or between clinical supervisors and supervisees. Beginning in the 1980s, the counseling profession became increasingly concerned with the ethical issues inherent in establishing appropriate boundaries. Much has been written since then about the harm that results when mental health professionals enter into sexual relationships with their clients. Throughout the 1980s, sexual misconduct received a great deal of attention in the professional literature, and the dangers of sexual relationships between counselor and client, professor and student, and supervisor and supervisee have been well documented.

Today there is clear and unanimous agreement that sexual relationships with clients, students, and supervisees are unethical, and prohibitions against them have been translated into ethics codes and law. Therapists who are found guilty of sexual misconduct face a range of negative consequences, including being the target of a lawsuit, being convicted of a felony, having their license revoked or suspended by the state, being expelled from their professional organization, losing their insurance coverage, and losing their job. The most recent ethics codes of professional organizations have added standards prohibiting sexual activity between supervisors and supervisees and also between faculty and students.

Today's students are being taught how to apply reasoning and an ethical decision-making model to address a host of ethical dilemmas. When I was teaching students in human services and counseling in the early 1970s, very few programs required a course in professional ethics. At best, ethics might have been given brief coverage in a course such as internship. Today most programs require a course in ethical, legal, and professional issues in counseling, and licensed mental health practitioners are typically required to take at least a full day workshop in ethics and the law every year or two as a condition for renewal of their license. Until the late 1980s, few textbooks or journal articles on ethics were being published. Today the standards of ethical practice and ethics codes are given prominence.

In my graduate program, there were no courses on supervision and no training in how to provide supervision. A great deal of attention is paid today to the quality of clinical supervision, including developing standards and formal training in supervision. Doctoral students now take a course in supervision, and their work with master's students is supervised.

Another main change I see in the counseling field is the expectation that counselors can competently deal with crisis situations and with clients who present with traumatic backgrounds. Treatment for individuals coping with trauma or intense crises is sorely needed, and this is a welcome shift in crisis treatment for a range of situations. A popular emerging subfield in the mental health professions is disaster mental health counseling, which places counseling professionals at the forefront of disaster response efforts. Many beginning counselors have reported feeling overwhelmed with the demands of crisis work. Coursework experiences can teach students how crisis situations affect their clients and can teach students how to counsel people in crisis.

The technology revolution has increased the reach of counselors through distance counseling, teaching online, and supervising via some form of technology. Counseling services can now reach clients in rural areas or at a distance wherever they may be, but I have concerns about increasingly relying on these methods, especially when this replaces face-to-face encounters. However, technology can supplement services that have been traditionally delivered.

There is a greater recognition today that the quality of the therapeutic relationship is a key determining factor leading to positive outcomes in therapy, regardless of a practitioner's theoretical orientation. More counseling professionals are agreeing that it is the human relationship that heals and brings about change. Abundant recent research has shown that the therapeutic relationship is more important than the techniques counselors use or the theory they embrace. Counselors should take their own personal development seriously and highlight relationship factors in their counseling process.

Another trend I see now is the increasing number of graduate students attending national, state, and regional professional conferences. During my graduate program, faculty did not suggest that students attend professional conferences, much less submit proposals to present at these conferences. It is good to see so many graduate students attending and presenting at conferences, sometimes on joint projects with their professors. The graduate students and new professionals I encounter at conferences demonstrate a particular interest and commitment to social justice issues. I am impressed with the vitality, creativity, and leadership of the generation of emerging scholars and practitioners.

For further reading on the topics discussed in this chapter, see *ACA Ethical Standards Casebook* (Herlihy & Corey, 2015a) and *Boundary Issues in Counseling: Multiple Roles and Responsibilities* (Herlihy & Corey, 2015b). For a more detailed discussion of the role of the therapeutic relationship in outcomes of treatments, see *Psychotherapy Relationships That Work: Evidence-Based Therapist Contributions* (Norcross & Lambert, 2019) and *Psychotherapy Relationships That Work: Evidence-Based Responsiveness* (Norcross & Wampold, 2019).

What are some of the biggest challenges facing the counseling profession today?

Our world is increasingly complex, and there are many sources of human suffering in this global village. Perhaps the main challenge counselors face today is how to inspire their clients to find meaning in life, which at times can seem absurd. More than ever, we need to help individuals learn how to love and appreciate themselves and how to actively reach out in loving and compassionate ways to others. Hatred, polarization in society, negativity and violence toward people who are different, lack of concern and compassion for others, and callous attitudes and behaviors have increased in recent years. A major task facing the counseling profession is helping clients replace indifference and even hatred with a loving concern for others. Counselors can do a great deal to facilitate changes with individuals, groups, and communities, and small changes can reverberate into larger changes. But I believe the mandate for counselors is far broader than the narrow focus on the problems our clients bring to us. Although most people seek therapy to better deal with particular problems, underlying many of these problems are existential concerns such as creating a life that is worth living.

What predictions do you have for the future of the counseling profession?

Weather predictions are often inaccurate, and my predictions for the future of the counseling profession are likely to be less accurate than any weather prediction. Counselors certainly want to understand the unfolding trends so they can prepare for the changing times that lie ahead. If I am pressed to gaze into a crystal ball, I predict that counselors will be increasingly called upon to help people and communities find creative approaches to cope with the many new disasters that are on the horizon. It is an understatement to say that we are increasingly plagued with natural disasters and human-caused disasters in our stressful world. Increasing numbers of people will need professional assistance to deal with these crisis situations. Natural disasters such as hurricanes, severe droughts, wildfires, earthquakes, and floods are devastating communities. Our planet is facing an unprecedented crisis of global warming and rising sea levels that threaten coastal cities. Human-caused disasters are increasing and causing anxiety and stress at a level that was unknown a few decades ago. These crises are taking an immense toll on human lives. Added to these horrific realities is the unresolved hatred and divisiveness present in our nation, the ever-present threat of wars, and daily examples of violence and aggression. Global catastrophic events bombard us daily, and we often numb ourselves to defend against these overwhelming painful realities.

I predict that disaster mental health counseling will expand in the near future. First-line responders will need therapy themselves as they continue responding to more frequent disasters. Many mental health workers are doing an incredible job of providing relief and healing to survivors of these unfortunate events, and it is important to acknowledge the positive impact counselors are having on so many. We must not give up hope of finding even small ways to address these enormous problems.

For more on how the counseling profession is dealing with the trauma associated with the crises in our world, I recommend *Disaster Mental Health Counseling: A Guide to Preparing and Responding* (Webber & Mascari, 2018), *Disaster Mental Health Counseling: Responding to Trauma in a Multicultural Context* (Stebnicki, 2017), and *Coping Skills for a Stressful World: A Workbook for Counselors and Clients* (Muratori & Haynes, 2020).

Reflection Questions

1. When you think of your emerging and future career in counseling, what is your mission?
2. What are the biggest challenges for the counseling profession today?
3. What predictions for the future of counseling would you like to see become a reality?
4. How do you expect the technological revolution to affect your work as a counselor?
5. Ethics in counseling practice is increasingly being given attention in graduate programs. In your own program, what kinds of ethical issues are you exploring?

Chapter 6

The Counselor as a Person

Introduction

The life experiences, attitudes, and caring that you bring to your practice are crucial factors in establishing an effective therapeutic relationship. Although knowledge and technical skill are essential, establishing a good working relationship with clients is of paramount importance in becoming an effective counselor. This section deals with the theme of the counselor as a person, which is central to developing your ability to function optimally as a professional.

• • •

What personal characteristics are needed to become an effective counselor?

Personal qualities and characteristics of counselors are significant in creating a therapeutic alliance with clients. There is no ideal combination of characteristics, and a wide range of people have become competent counselors. Consider the following attributes and reflect on how these characteristics apply to you. To my way of thinking, it is important for counselors to establish and develop these attributes in both their personal and professional life:

- Being aware of your strengths and weaknesses
- Being authentic, sincere, and honest
- Being able to show up and be fully present
- Having a curiosity and openness to learning
- Demonstrating courage in pursuing your passions and dreams
- Being sincerely interested in the welfare of others and caring for others
- Acquiring interpersonal skills, such as empathy and self-disclosure, to form a working alliance with clients
- Replacing negative self-judgments with understanding, acceptance, and encouragement
- Having compassion for yourself and treating yourself with kindness
- Accepting and welcoming differences in social class, race, ethnicity, creed, gender, ability, and sexual/affectional orientation
- Developing and refining your attentive and listening skills
- Being able to self-disclose appropriately
- Having the ability to foster trust with clients
- Taking care of yourself in all respects
- Striving to be humble and avoiding arrogance
- Having a healthy sense of self-love and pride

This list of characteristics is meant to stimulate your thinking about the personality traits you would like to develop or might find essential as an effective counselor. Your willingness to struggle to become a more therapeutic person is of the utmost importance. The more you are willing to work on your personal development, the better counselor you will become.

In what ways are the counselor as a person and as a professional related, and how do they influence one another?

It is not possible to talk about the counselor as a professional without considering who the counselor is as a person. Who you are as a *person* and as a *professional* are intertwined facets that cannot be separated. My experience has convinced me that our beliefs, values, personal characteristics, level of personal functioning, and our way of being in the world greatly influence the quality of our functioning as counseling professionals. Who you are as a person and the quality of the client-counselor relationship are the most important variables that contribute to successful therapy. You bring your human qualities and the life experiences that have influenced you into every counseling session. In your training program, you will acquire knowledge about the theories of counseling, learn assessment and intervention techniques, and acquire and refine a wide range of intervention skills. Although knowledge and skills are necessary, they are not sufficient for establishing and maintaining an effective therapeutic relationship. If you expect to promote change in your clients, you need to be open to change in your own life. Your willingness to live in accordance with what you teach and thus to be a positive model for your clients is what makes you a therapeutic person.

For more on the topic of the counselor as a person and as a professional, see *Creating Your Professional Path: Lessons From My Journey* (Corey, 2010) and *Issues and Ethics in the Helping Professions* (Corey, Corey, & Corey, 2019). For a more detailed discussion of the person of the counselor, see *Psychotherapy Relationships That Work: Evidence-Based Therapist Contributions* (Norcross & Lambert, 2019) and *Psychotherapy Relationships That Work: Evidence-Based Responsiveness* (Norcross & Wampold, 2019).

How can I recognize and best manage my client's transference to me and my countertransference reactions to clients?

Transference includes any feelings clients project onto their counselor, whether the source of these feelings is from past or present relationships. Transference allows clients to understand and resolve unfinished business from past relationships through their present relationship with their counselor. Clients bring unresolved feelings with significant others into the therapeutic relationship and project them onto you, which distorts the way your clients perceive and react to you as their counselor. Rather than trying to avoid transference reactions, welcome this as an opportunity for clients to work through a similar emotional conflict from their past in their relationship with you. This process can reduce the effects of their early negative experiences. You need to understand what transference means, how your clients may view you in light of their past experiences, and how to deal with transference skillfully and therapeutically.

When your clients manifest transference toward you, this can evoke reactions within you. *Countertransference* occurs when you are triggered into emotional reactivity or respond defensively or lose your ability to be present in a relationship because your own dynamics have become involved. When you encounter clients you perceive as being problematic, reflect on your reactions and what they are bringing out in you rather than zeroing in on their problematic behaviors. The emotionally intense relationships that develop can be expected to bring your unresolved conflicts to the surface. It is crucial for you to be aware of how your personal dynamics may affect what is taking place in your therapeutic relationships. Recognizing the signs of your countertransference is a key step in preventing a counterproductive impact in working with your clients. When you are aware of your personal triggers, the chances increase that you will be able to manage your countertransference appropriately.

I have found that students tend to fear countertransference to such a degree that they are reluctant to tell their supervisors about it. You can use all of your reactions in therapeutic ways, so countertransference is not necessarily problematic. You must become aware of the sources of your countertransference to use it effectively. Countertransference becomes problematic when it is not recognized, understood, monitored, and managed. Your countertransference reactions can provide valuable information for both you and your client. If you are able to use your own feelings as a way of understanding yourself, your client, and the relationship between the two of you, these feelings can be a positive and healing force. In my experience, countertransference is a rich source of information about how our clients might affect the people in their lives. Something therapeutic can often be found through an honest exploration of countertransference. It is not realistic to assume that you will be able to eliminate countertransference completely, but you can learn to recognize manifestations of countertransference as part of *your personal dynamics* rather than as your client's problem.

For a more complete understanding of countertransference, see Chapter 11 in *The Making of a Therapist* (Cozolino, 2004).

When is crying in a session appropriate?

The answer to this question hinges on *who is crying* in the session, the client or the counselor. When clients are crying, I generally assume that their tears are triggered by some emotions, such as sadness, some unfinished business, recalling traumatic events, a release of painful feelings, and even sometimes joy. Give clients space to experience whatever is emotionally activating them. It is not your role to give clients advice, to reassure them, to get them to shift their attention to a more comfortable topic, or to get them to stop crying. You can be therapeutic by being present for clients and encouraging them to express verbally what they are experiencing when they are able to do so. In therapeutic groups that my colleagues and I facilitated, group members often experienced a catharsis as they recalled and shared painful events from their past. Crying in these group sessions was not a problem, and members typically reported how much lighter and freer they felt after releasing pent-up feelings. As we facilitated these groups, we were often emotionally affected by members' emotional releases, but this did not interfere with our ability to remain psychologically present and to function effectively as group therapists.

If you find yourself emotionally moved while in session with a client who is crying, share how you are being emotionally affected by being with the person. Even in situations like this, it is important to keep the focus on the client. If you find that you frequently experience an intense range of feelings when your clients are expressing emotions, especially by crying, it is a good idea to bring this into your supervision sessions. Clients who are crying may be tapping into your own unfinished business, which can be a manifestation of countertransference. Your supervisor can help you identify the emotions surfacing in you and can help you gain awareness of how this is affecting your ability to connect with the client. Your personal counseling session is a good place to explore why you are getting lost in a client's story.

How do you learn to control your emotions when you are with a client who activates your personal issues?

In your work as a counselor, you are not simply facilitating a healing process with your clients, you are also gaining a deeper understanding of your own dynamics. As you attend to your clients' stories, you help them explore their human concerns in more depth. Pay attention to what it is like for you to be in this immediate relationship. Clients may trigger something in you, and you may be surprised by these emotions. When this happens, let your clients know that you are responding emotionally to what you are hearing, but do so without going into detail about your own life experiences.

If a client is expressing intense sadness in recounting a traumatic event, you might be triggered by feeling sadness of your own, even though you may not have shared a similar experience. This does not necessarily mean that countertransference is occurring. It could simply be that you are affected by being with the client and are feeling empathy toward the person. If you find that you are often triggered by the emotional expressions of your clients, this could be a manifestation of your own unfinished business. Your personal therapy will be of the utmost importance in learning how to identify your emotional reactions and how to manage them. Finally, if your client is sobbing and you are sobbing, this might well be a countertransference matter that you should consider exploring in supervision or personal therapy.

When you have had intense emotional experiences with clients all day, how do you unwind and not carry your work home?

It is often difficult for beginning counselors to disengage from clients and to manage the psychological impact of this work. This is especially true if counselors are seeing high-risk individuals, clients who are working through traumatic events, or clients who are highly emotional. We certainly need to have empathy for our clients and to connect with them, but we also need to disconnect at the end of the session. This is easier said than done. It is natural to be concerned about your clients, and emotionally separating yourself from them takes practice. Clients must be free to experience emotional pain and to express it in session because this is a critical part of working through a traumatic event. It may help if you can reframe a client's expression of pain as a path for healing.

If you are a beginning counselor, in supervision you can talk not only about your clients but also about reactions they are bringing up in you. In some cases, your stress and preoccupation with them may be due to countertransference reactions. If you are getting overly involved in the traumatic stories of your clients, use your personal therapy sessions to learn how to emotionally detach from individuals you are counseling. Doing your personal work is critical in being able to separate yourself from the problem-saturated and painful stories of clients.

Be patient with yourself as you learn to refrain from bringing the painful stories you hear in the office into your daily life. It helps to have other interests separate from your work, and engaging in rejuvenating activities can enable you to unwind after an intense day of being with others. You may enjoy cooking, and this could be a way for you to leave your work at the office. Other things you can do involve writing in your journal, reading a novel, playing a musical instrument, doing art work, or watching a movie. Engage in activities that are enjoyable for you, and realize that you deserve this down time. You won't be able to be therapeutic with your clients if you burden yourself with their emotional experiences and concerns when you arrive home. If you are having difficulty leaving your work at the office, don't be too hard on yourself. You are just learning the art of counseling, and it will take time to learn to disconnect from the problem-saturated stories of your clients. You can best take care of those you are counseling if you have a life apart from being a counselor and if you are taking steps to prevent empathy fatigue.

Are there risks of becoming too invested in your concern for your clients? Is there such a thing as caring too much?

We need to be able to let ourselves care about our clients, to listen to the stories they need to tell, and to express our compassion, but we also need to let them leave us psychologically when they leave the session physically. For example, if we identify too closely with a client's painful story, we won't be able to make interventions that can be healing. We can enter our clients' world and convey our understanding and empathy, which can be extremely therapeutic, but it is imperative not to blur the distinction between their world and our own world. When I first began counseling individuals, I often felt compassion for them, and their life stories were engaging. It was not easy for me to disengage from certain clients after they left a session. Talking with colleagues about being overly concerned and having difficulty detaching was useful in helping me gain a different perspective. Eventually, I had less trouble letting clients go back into their daily life at the end of a session.

We need to be invested in our clients' struggles, but we do not do them a favor if we do more work than they are doing. We are useful to our clients when we are working to put ourselves out of business. Our job is to provide our clients with tools to use in making decisions for how they want to live. We need to have faith that our clients have the capacity to make significant life decisions, and we need to have trust in our ability to encourage their autonomy.

Interesting reading on some of the topics covered in this chapter can be found in *Letters to a Young Therapist* (Pipher, 2003), *The Gift of Therapy* (Yalom, 2003), and *Lying on the Couch* (Yalom, 1997).

Reflection Questions

1. What characteristics are crucial to being an effective counselor?
2. How do you see who you are as a person related to who you can become as a professional?
3. When a friend confides in you about a serious problem, how do you typically react? Do you simply listen and be supportive? Try to help your friend find a solution? Try to solve the problem for your friend? The way you react with a friend may be a clue to understanding how you will react with clients.
4. To what degree are you concerned that the intense emotions of your clients will affect you personally? What ideas do you have to psychologically leave your work at the end of a day?
5. Can you identify one manifestation of countertransference on your part? What would this be? How can you best deal with your countertransference reactions?

Chapter 7

Personal Therapy

Introduction

You don't need to be free of all problems to effectively counsel others, but you do need to be aware of how your personal issues might affect your work with clients. Old emotional wounds may surface when you begin working with clients. If you are in personal counseling during your internship, bring any unresolved issues into your therapy sessions to process difficulties you are experiencing in your life. Your experience of personal therapy will increase your appreciation for the courage clients show in their therapeutic journey. There is no better way to learn about the counseling process than to experience it as a client. Many training programs require counselors-in-training to obtain their own counseling. Do you think participating in your own therapeutic experience would be valuable? If you have been a client in personal therapy, what has this experience been like for you?

• • •

Is it important to participate in my own therapy in addition to receiving support from family and friends? What are the benefits of personal therapy for me as a counseling student?

Having good relationships with family members and close friends is extremely important. They can be a source of nurturance for you and provide a buffer against the stresses of this demanding professional work. If an internship experience is part of your training program, your work with clients may bring some unexpressed and unresolved feelings to the surface. Do not be surprised if earlier emotional wounds are reopened through intensive work with your clients. Personal therapy is a valuable component for exploring your life in some depth. You can bring psychological issues that are emerging for you in your work to your own therapy sessions.

Personal therapy is valuable for both trainees and seasoned professionals. Participating in personal psychotherapy on a periodic basis is a self-care strategy that may help you maintain your competence throughout your career. Personal therapy can be instrumental in expanding your awareness of transference and countertransference processes, increasing your empathy and compassion for your clients, and becoming self-aware so you can manage your emotional reactions when working with clients. In addition, self-reflection will reduce the likelihood of burnout and eventual impairment. Perhaps most important, being a client will keep you humble. Many of my students have been in therapy, and they attest to its value in understanding how their past plays a role in their current behavior. Counselors can benefit from personal therapy at different stages of their life throughout their career.

My own personal therapy was instrumental in identifying my personal issues and learning to manage my countertransference. Growing up I experienced my father as being both depressed and anxious, which resulted in me working hard to cheer him up and to get him to laugh. His depressed moods and behavior scared me, and that has had a significant impact on me to this day, both personally and professionally. To avoid both depression and anxiety, I kept a very busy schedule, rarely taking time to simply sit and reflect on my day. Keeping depression at bay has been operative in my life since childhood. When I began working as a counselor in a university counseling center, I encouraged depressed clients to make an appointment with another counselor on the staff. My personal therapy taught me that counseling depressed clients was difficult for me because of my reluctance to deal with my own fears of depression. If I allowed myself to enter the world of these depressed clients, I was afraid of being overwhelmed by depression. Recognizing my ways of coping with my fears taught me the important lesson that I could not take clients in any direction that I had not been willing to explore in my own life. Had I not challenged my fears and countertransference, I would have continued to avoid any topics that clients wanted to explore that were anxiety-provoking for me. My personal therapy was beneficial for me in many ways in addition to dealing with countertransference issues. I think I learned to have more patience with clients who struggle to make progress. Without a doubt, my own therapy has been a key factor in learning to accept myself and to be more compassionate, which has translated into increasing my compassion with clients.

Alternative routes to personal development include reflecting on the meaning of your life and work, reading and journal writing, participating in peer groups, remaining open to the feedback and reactions of significant people in your life, engaging in spiritual activities such as meditating, participating in physical challenges, and spending time with your family and friends.

For further readings on being a client and how to get the most from therapy, see *On Being a Therapist* (Kottler, 2017), and for a rationale for therapists to engage in personal therapy, see *The Gift of Therapy* (Yalom, 2003).

Should counseling programs require trainees to participate in their own counseling?

I admit to a definite bias regarding whether training programs should require students to participate in their own therapy. If I were a director of a training program, I would require personal therapy as a vital part of a student's experience. Learning from books and classes is valuable, but therapeutic experiences provide both self-knowledge and opportunities to learn about the counseling process by being a recipient of experiential work. A rationale for this requirement rests on the assumption that we cannot take our clients further in their journey than we have gone ourselves. I think programs have a responsibility to ensure that students can gain access to therapy, such as finding therapists in the community who are willing to offer students affordable rates for counseling services.

I am particularly in favor of encouraging participation in a personal growth group or some type of experiential group as a way for trainees to learn about themselves and how to use counseling skills effectively. A major benefit to students who participate in an experiential group is the opportunity to identify personal characteristics that might enhance or inhibit their ability to function as future counselors. A group experience is not an appropriate place to work through unfinished business from your past, but the group can serve you by sensitizing you to how your vulnerabilities and your potential countertransference issues could interfere with your work as a counselor. If you participate in an experiential group as a part of your training, you can use your experience for personal change and also for working on your ability to be an effective counselor. Members of your group can help you take an honest look at yourself and help you better understand how you come across to them.

When do you think someone's work in therapy is finished?

Early in the course of a therapy experience, clients identify clear and specific goals that guide the treatment process. Once the client and the therapist agree that these goals have been achieved, the therapeutic journey is at an end unless the client identifies new goals. Clients are invited to consider returning to counseling months or even years later to deal with future life adjustment or developmental challenges.

Many therapists believe that their primary function is to assist clients in becoming their own therapists. Clients learn skills that they can apply to future problems. In brief therapy, practitioners are actively involved from the initial meeting, and clients are aware that therapy is a short-term process. Counselors summarize and evaluate each session and devise homework to be carried out by clients between sessions. In general, therapy ends when both therapist and client agree that terminating is in order. However, clients have the option of returning to therapy at a later date if they feel it would be beneficial.

To what extent do you see yourself as experiencing your own therapy when you are being a therapist to another?

When I am counseling others, I am not engaged in doing my own therapy with them. However, I experience significant personal benefits in my therapeutic work. Our clients often serve as mirrors for us, and providing therapy to others opens us to our own existential concerns and life choices. Therapy is a collaborative venture in which both my clients and I will be transformed if I allow myself to be touched by life.

I like the idea embodied in the relationship-oriented approaches to psychotherapy of therapists being fellow travelers with clients. When I facilitate clients who are engaging in deep self-exploration, I am invariably drawn into discussions of existential themes such as mortality, the meaning in life, freedom, responsibility, anxiety, and aloneness. I need to resonate with my clients' experiences and struggle to face life honestly. This capacity for resonance requires me to take part in the therapeutic encounter in a fully engaged manner.

Reflection Questions

1. Have you experienced being the client and receiving personal therapy? What was this like for you? How do you think your own therapy affects you as a counselor-in-training?
2. If you were to seek personal therapy, what qualities would you look for in selecting a therapist?
3. How would you react if your program required you to participate in your own therapy?
4. What do you think of engaging in personal therapy on a periodic basis as a self-care strategy to maintain your competence throughout your career? In what ways do you think being a client in therapy can make you a better counselor?
5. What are your thoughts about being in an experiential group, or a process group, as a part of your program?

Chapter 8

Self-Care and Wellness

Introduction

Wellness embodies a great deal more than the absence of illness. It is the result of a conscious commitment to care for ourselves on all human dimensions. Achieving wellness requires diligent work, but this is a most rewarding path that leads to peace and vitality. A holistic approach to wellness requires that we pay attention to the specific aspects of our lifestyle, including how we work and play, how we relax, what we eat, how we keep physically fit, our relationships with self and others, our values and beliefs, and our spiritual practices.

Self-care consists of the actions we take to improve our health and better meet the many challenges of being an effective counselor. Self-care is an ethical imperative for counselors; it protects us from burnout, empathy fatigue, impairment, and other conditions that can detract from our effectiveness. If you commit to a self-care action plan during your graduate program and at an early stage in your professional development, maintaining your self-care program as you get older will not be overwhelming. This is a good time to reflect on how satisfied you are with your self-care and what changes you would most want to make in various aspects of your life.

• • •

Why is self-care an ethical mandate for graduate students and counseling professionals?

I feel passionate about self-care for both students and counseling professionals. I am seriously committed to taking care of myself in all respects. I would not have the stamina required to keep up with my professional endeavors if I did not practice self-care on a regular basis. I enjoy experiencing the natural world each day, hiking and bike riding, and participating in activities that bring meaning to my life. Because of my commitment to self-care, I have been able to engage in my life's work without experiencing burnout. My work has been fulfilling and has provided the foundation for my purpose in life, which includes providing service in many ways, especially through teaching and writing books.

For an in-depth and comprehensive treatment of counselor self-care, I recommend *Leaving It at the Office: A Guide to Psychotherapist Self-Care* (Norcross & VandenBos, 2018) and *Counselor Self-Care* (Corey, Muratori, Austin, & Austin, 2018).

How can I manage self-care when I don't have the time?

Ongoing attention to self-care is essential for preventing burnout and for maintaining psychological wellness. If you neglect self-care, you will not have the energy necessary to be present for your clients. Self-care is an ethical imperative, but I hope you do not think it is just one more burden to add to the list of your already busy life. Self-care does not need to consume an inordinate amount of time, nor does it have to be expensive. During the day, take a brief walk, spend 10 minutes in quiet reflection, or take a 10-minute nap. Find self-care activities that you enjoy and that will assist you in retaining your vitality.

I encourage students to set self-care goals that are realistic and meaningful for them, and I urge them to be patient as they pursue their goals. Now is the time to begin taking better care of yourself in all respects if you hope to succeed, not only in graduate school but also during your early professional career. In my ethics class, students explore the personal meaning of the ethical imperative of self-care and discuss ways they can address changes in all aspects of their daily life. They see the value of reaching out to fellow students as a support system to help them implement their plan and to keep them accountable. My students feel pride in what they *are doing* rather than dwelling on what they *are not doing.* You must find the self-care practices that work for you.

How can we recognize when we are on a path toward burnout?

Burnout is a condition of physical, emotional, and mental exhaustion that results from constant or repeated pressure associated with an intense, long-term involvement with people with intense needs. Burnout is also associated with a sense of helplessness, a negative view of self, and negative attitudes toward work, life, and other people. Burnout begins slowly and progresses through several stages, it typically results in personal feelings of depression, loss of morale, feelings of isolation, depersonalization, and reduced productivity.

In the beginning of your counseling career, you are likely to be motivated by a sense of idealism. As you experience the inevitable frustrations and stresses of being a counselor, you may be challenged to find ways to cope effectively with the stresses of work. Factors that may place you on a path toward burnout include unrealistic work demands, poor working conditions, lack of control, lack of support, and insufficient rewards. It may not be possible to quit working or to change jobs, but you can change how you are approaching your work. Attitudinal shifts can make a big difference in keeping burnout at bay. Take time to evaluate what you are doing, and be open to making even small changes in the activities that are draining your energy. These small changes can lead to bigger changes. Take an inventory of your personal life and look for areas that you might want to change. If you are not having enough fun, what can you do to change this? If you have lost contact with your friends and family members, what are you willing to do to reconnect? Too often counselors are reluctant to recognize that they need help, or they are unwilling to ask for support from others. Burnout is often associated with a sense of isolation, and a remedy is to make connections with people you can reach out to for feedback and support. This might be a mentor, a teacher, a supervisor, a close friend, a relative, a peer, or a support group.

How do you continue to do what you do and avoid burnout?

I can honestly say that I have never reached a stage of burnout. I have certainly experienced stress in carrying out my professional responsibilities, and sometimes these stresses are manifested in body symptoms such as headaches and fatigue. When I realized I was attempting to do too many things at once, I had to learn the value of carefully reflecting on the pros and cons of taking on new projects. Many of my personal needs were met from my involvement in projects, but I came to realize that I couldn't do everything I was offered even though I enjoyed all of it. I learned the value of making a personal assessment in determining what changes I needed to make to sustain my vitality in my private life as well as my professional life. Making these key decisions has enabled me to stave off burnout.

Taking self-care seriously has been my best strategy for preventing burnout and keeping me vital. I am convinced that prevention is better than remediation. Over the years I have learned how essential clarity of purpose, motivation, and self-discipline are for engaging in productive work. As I mentor students, I frequently talk with them about establishing priorities and learning practical strategies for managing stress and preventing burnout. I encourage them to reflect on how their professional or academic life affects their personal relationships, as well as the impact it has on clients.

What are the best ways to prevent burnout? What should you do if you experience symptoms of burnout?

Self-care is best viewed as an ongoing preventive activity for all mental health practitioners. If you are engaging in various forms of self-care, you have a good chance of successfully meeting the demands of your professional work. It is of paramount importance that you become attuned to the warning signals that you are being depleted, and take seriously your own need for nurturing and for sustaining yourself. If you pay attention to the early warning signs and develop practical strategies for keeping burnout at bay, you will be better able to respond effectively to the challenges your work presents. If you have a pattern of putting others' needs before your own, you increase the chances of burnout. By proactively engaging in taking care of yourself on all levels, you increase the odds of preventing burnout. Here are some suggestions for you to consider.

- Assess what you are doing and whether this is working for you: "Is what I am doing realistic? If I continue at this pace, will I eventually experience burnout?" Reflect on these questions and decide what specific behaviors you may want to change.
- Take time each day to do something you enjoy, even for a short time.
- Simply because you *can* do something does not mean you *should* do something.
- Recognize that no matter how much you have to offer, there is a limit to what you can give to others. Know your limits and communicate them to others.
- Find sources of meaning outside of your work and educational program.
- Consider the hazards of the work you choose. Talk to others in that line of work about how they handle their work stress. If it is a high-stress position, think about ways you can educate and immunize yourself from the stress associated with the work. For example, working in a forensic setting, trauma center, suicide service, domestic violence treatment center, rape recovery program, drug rehabilitation program, program for treating seriously mentally ill, or a posttraumatic stress disorder program is typically associated with considerable stress, which increases the risk of burnout and impairment.
- Accept the fact that either you control your stress or it controls you. Pay attention to what your body, mind, and spirit need in order to effectively deal with stress. This might include a combination of physical activity, rest and relaxation, contact with significant others, adequate diet and nutrition, cultivation of hobbies, doing more of what gives your life meaning, and some form of mindfulness practice.
- It is easy to become overwhelmed if you are preoccupied with things you feel powerless to change. Instead, concentrate on the aspects of your life that you have the power to change.
- The companionship of colleagues and fellow students can be a great asset to you, both personally and professionally. Make the effort to create a support group that can provide you with encouragement.
- Recognize any early signs of burnout, and take steps to deal with this syndrome. Devote your energies toward preventing this condition rather than waiting to treat it once it becomes more severe.

We make many decisions each day that are either life-enhancing or life-depleting. Make an accurate self-assessment on a daily basis, then make concrete changes in your self-care practices. Changes do not have to be made all at once; decide to live more intentionally one day at a time.

For a more in-depth discussion on preventing burnout, see *Burnout: The Cost of Caring* (Maslach, 2015).

Why is it important to create a self-care action plan?

You cannot provide nourishment to your clients if you don't nourish yourself. Even though you may not reach an ideal level of self-care, working toward this goal will yield positive results. Many of us want to change some of our self-care patterns but resist designing an action plan that will lead to basic changes. Good intentions are not enough. In various aspects of my life, I have discovered that the key to success is designing a realistic plan. When it comes to self-care, I know my plans keep me on course, and I regularly evaluate how my plans are working.

Formulate a specific and realistic plan that will enable you to establish a more satisfying life. In the classes I teach, I give significant attention to the importance of self-care. My students know that relapses may happen, but that does not stop them from continuing with their action plan. It is good to see that most of them are not overly self-critical when their plan is not working well. They are willing to accept lapses and forgive themselves, realizing that being kind to themselves is better than being self-critical. Not only does focusing on implementing self-care patterns enable them to succeed in their graduate program, but they report positive changes in their personal lives. Be willing to evaluate your plan and modify it as necessary. The commitment you make now puts you on a path toward a more meaningful professional career.

A useful book on creating realistic action plans is *Reality Therapy and Self-Evaluation: The Key to Client Change* (Wubbolding, 2017).

What tips do you have about managing time?

I have often been asked how I manage to keep up with my diverse professional commitments. My usual reply is that I greatly enjoy most of my professional endeavors and find meaning in my work. I believe that the way I choose to use my time is a good indicator of what I value. I do realize that everything takes time and that time is a valuable resource that enables me to do what I want in my life. I have learned how important it is to be organized, to set realistic goals, and to identify steps to accomplish these goals. Figuring out my priorities is as crucial to me as monitoring how I am spending the time I have.

Students consistently tell me that they experience an increased level of stress as the semester progresses, mainly because many projects are due at the same time and they have not planned effectively. Most students work and have family obligations as well, and they struggle to balance these multiple roles. I tell my students who are interested in making better use of their time that a good place to begin is by monitoring how they are spending their time. Doing this helps them make conscious choices about how they can best attend to the multiple roles they play in their school, work, and personal life. There is no one best way to budget your time; you will need to find a system that works for you.

Time management is a key strategy in managing stress and in taking care of ourselves, but time management is not an end in itself. Consider the following questions to see if your time management program is beginning to control you rather than you being in control of it. This is a sign that it is time to reevaluate and reset your priorities. Consider these questions as you review your time management plan.

- Am I interested in creating a self-care program that enables me to keep a balanced life?
- Do I make the time to take care of myself?
- Am I able to establish clear and attainable goals? Do I reevaluate my goals periodically?
- Do I generally accomplish what I have set out to do each day?
- Am I able to incorporate fun with work?
- Do I frequently feel rushed and try to accomplish too much in too short of a time?
- Before accepting new projects, do I think about how realistic it is to fit one more project or activity into my already busy schedule? Am I able to say no to a request without feeling guilty?
- Instead of doing everything myself, am I willing to ask for help from others and learn to delegate?
- Do I make time for nurturing my significant relationships?
- Do I create time for quiet reflection on what I am doing and how satisfied I am with my choices?

- Do I wish I had used my time differently today than I did yesterday? Last week? Last month?

Much of the daily stress we experience is probably due to our inability to say no to certain requests or invitations. If you say yes but are unable to honor your commitment, disappointment in yourself is the likely result. Another source of misusing time is procrastinating. Putting things off, especially if they need immediate attention, only compounds the problem rather than being a solution. In the long run, procrastination tends to lead to disappointment, feelings of failure, anxiety, and increased stress. Procrastination is not simply the result of lacking time management skills. On a deeper level, procrastinating can be associated with the fear of failure or, in some cases, the fear of success. Ask yourself if the tasks you are putting off are meaningful to you. You may decide that certain projects do not warrant your time after all.

Failing to maintain a realistic schedule results in frustration and anxiety, and tasks simply do not get done. Using a daily, weekly, monthly, and yearly planner or composing a daily to-do list may help you create an effective schedule. Making a commitment to another person about staying on schedule with a project will motivate you to do your part on time. Checking in with this person also provides an opportunity to discuss any problems that may arise.

Personally, I have never missed a deadline in turning in a book to the publisher. In fact, I generally submit manuscripts before the due dates. This does not happen by accident but by careful planning and time management. I still struggle with trying to do more in a given day than is realistic. I often have a dozen things on my to-do list for a day, and I am generally lucky if I am able to check off half of them. Unscheduled events often prevent me from finishing what was on my daily agenda. I am still learning to evaluate requests that come my way and decline them if time and energy do not allow me to do a good job. There is no perfect way to manage time, and you will need to find a way that works best for you.

What is resilience, and how can I become more resilient?

Resilience is the ability of an individual to effectively cope with adversity from extraordinarily stressful and adverse events while maintaining a positive outlook. Resilient individuals are able to act in adaptive ways to various crises and traumatic situations. People who have experienced a crisis or disaster have often found inner strength and resources they did not know they had. Some individuals experience growth following a catastrophic situation, gaining mastery and confidence that will enable them to successfully handle future disasters and crises as well. Resilience includes some of the following characteristics:

- Adapting to difficulties, adversity, and traumatic experiences
- Accepting difficult life situations without giving up hope
- Successfully coping with stressful life events
- Enduring traumatic events without lasting harm

Most of us would like to think we will be able to remain calm, develop and implement an action plan, maintain a sense of hopefulness, and keep a sense of optimism during a major crisis. Some people seem to be inherently more resilient than others; however, resilience can be learned and developed. We all can practice and implement new skills to become more resilient. Here are a few ways you can become more resilient.

- Develop solid relationships with family members and friends. Connection to others and social support are critical in developing and maintaining resilience.
- Spend some time reflecting on your existing strengths and resources, and use this as a way to develop new strengths.
- Believe that you have the ability to deal with life's problems.
- Develop effective self-care practices that you can utilize following a crisis.
- Review past successes with coping or overcoming crises, and build on those successes for dealing with future crises.
- Learn from adversities and mistakes you have made.

If you increase your resilience, you will be better able to cope with the stresses that frequently lead to burnout. Taking care of yourself in all aspects of your life is one of the best ways to acquire resilience.

For building your own resilience, I highly recommend *Roadmap to Resilience: A Guide for Military, Trauma Victims and Their Families* (Meichenbaum, 2012) and *Coping Skills for a Stressful World: A Workbook for Counselors and Clients* (Muratori & Haynes, 2020).

How is self-compassion a route to caring for others?

Self-compassion involves being nonjudgmental, accepting, and kind to ourselves. At times in my life, I have been self-critical and wanted to be different. It took me a long time to realize that I could not make changes in my way of living until I accepted the way I was at the present time. Learning the art of self-compassion is a starting point for making life changes. If we hope to be kind to others, we must first be kind to ourselves. Compassion and love transform and elevate us. If we are able to be compassionate with ourselves, our compassion toward our significant others and toward our clients will increase. Be patient with your process as you learn to practice self-compassion.

Two resources I recommend on learning more about self-compassion are *Self-Compassion* (Neff, 2011) and *The Mindful Self-Compassion Workbook* (Neff & Germer, 2018).

How can spending time in nature enhance my physical and mental health?

Being in nature for some time each day is an invigorating experience. There are many benefits to spending time in nature, and many people find this to be a source of nourishment. I find that I am able to clear my mind and feel refreshed when I take a walk on a trail in the mountain community where I live most of the year. I greatly enjoy any opportunities I have to experience trees, animals, creeks, mountains, blue skies, and the ocean. Many of my ideas for books, classes, and other projects were conceived on a hiking trail! Since early in my career, being outdoors has been a major source of meaning and inspiration in my life.

It is more difficult to immerse ourselves in nature if we live in an urban area. If you find that urbanization and technology get in the way of experiencing what the world has to offer, you can still find some small space where you can take refuge. When I attend a professional conference in a large metropolitan location, I almost always find some place to escape from the hustle and bustle of the city. I usually discover a nearby park where I can retreat from the city noises.

Counselors are increasingly suggesting that their clients reconnect with nature. The Dalai Lama has suggested that wellness and happiness can be enhanced by spending at least 30 minutes a day in nature. I highly recommend that you schedule even a few minutes a day to get outside of your office and refresh yourself. See what a difference this can make in your life.

How can I re-create myself through recreation?

As much as you may be immersed in your work, you are likely to compromise your effectiveness as a counselor if you do not develop other interests as well. Even rewarding work expends energy; spending even a small amount of time away from work projects will likely increase your productivity. Work alone is not likely to take care of all of your needs. A challenge you will most likely face is balancing work, family, and leisure pursuits. There have been times when I was so immersed in my work that I did not cultivate interests in addition to work. I paid a price for not making adequate time for recreation, which led me to focus more attention on leisure pursuits. Because I live by the work ethic of accomplishing and producing, I have sometimes overlooked the value of living in the present moment and fully experiencing what is unfolding before me. By placing so much emphasis on *doing*, I continue to struggle in recognizing the value of *being*.

Recreation is key to creating a balanced life. Recreation involves engaging in behaviors that energize you or in creating new interests. You may think you don't have time for recreation, but even small breaks can be beneficial. Some of you will say that you cannot afford to go to a place you would love to visit, but many options cost nothing or are affordable. Think of hobbies you would like to cultivate, activities you would like to partake in more often, and small ways of bringing more fun and joy into your life. You probably can identify a range of activities that not only provide you with a break from work but also enhance your relationships with others. Making time for recreation is essential for re-creating yourself and freeing you from the stultifying routines that reduce your well-being. If you make recreation an enjoyable part of your life, you are bound to become a more interesting and effective counselor.

My students have said that their lives are so busy that they cannot afford to put leisure time into their schedule. When they do take time out and do something fun, some claim that they feel guilty. I encourage them to challenge this guilt rather than being ruled by it. Remind yourself that you *do deserve* to enjoy leisure time and to pursue avenues of recreation that will maintain your vitality.

A suggestion for learning more about many of the topics in this section, especially recreation and leisure, is *I Never Knew I Had a Choice* (Corey, Corey, & Muratori, 2018).

In what ways is developing a mindfulness approach to daily life fundamental in our personal life and in the practice of counseling?

A purposeful way of living involves doing one thing at a time and immersing ourselves in that experience. Through intentional practice we can learn to focus and to bring our attention back to the present moment when distractions intrude. Mindfulness practice clears the mind and calms the body, which enables us to focus on here-and-now awareness in a nonjudgmental way. A key part of this practice involves training ourselves to intentionally focus on our present experience with an attitude of curiosity and compassion. With practice, we can bring our attention to what we are presently experiencing rather than dwelling on the past or being preoccupied with the future. Mindfulness is not limited to periods of formal practice; rather, it is meant to become a way of life.

Living in the moment may seem like it should be relatively easy to accomplish, but it requires effort and discipline. To be honest, I have difficulty staying aware of what is unfolding for me moment by moment. My mind races here and there, and too often I miss what is right before me. When I am not engaged in being mindful, the consequences are often costly. A few years ago I damaged the side of my car by rushing when I was turning out of a parking garage. Looking at the side of my car was a good reminder that haste makes waste.

In hurrying and trying to do too many things at once, I have hurt myself physically as well. At an American Counseling Association conference, I was rushing down an escalator to a presentation I was scheduled to give when I realized that the room I was looking for was on the floor above me. Preoccupied with thinking about what I would say as an opening statement, I impetuously turned around and began running up the escalator. This proved to be a huge mistake. I tripped and reached out with my left arm to brace my fall, injuring my shoulder and upper arm. I got up and ran to the room and began my presentation by telling my audience of the "stupid thing" I had just done. When I returned home, an orthopedic specialist confirmed that I had fractured a bone in my arm and also for a time had a dislocated shoulder. He informed me that I was fortunate that I did not tear my rotator cuff, which he would expect 90% of the time with the kind of fall I experienced. This one act of mindlessness and rushing cost me dearly in physical pain, time, and money. This was a hard-earned lesson and another reminder to me to live mindfully, slow down, and focus on the present moment.

Being mindful in everyday living will better enable you to be fully present when counseling clients or engaging in other professional work. Mindfulness increases your capacity for presence, which is central to establishing and maintaining quality relationships with your clients. Reaping the benefits of living in the present, both personally and professionally, are well worth the effort we put forth.

A recommended resource for learning more about mindfulness is *The Healing Power of Mindfulness: A New Way of Being* (Kabat-Zinn, 2018).

How does the way we think affect our ability to manage stress?

It goes without saying that we live in a stress-filled world. It is to our advantage to learn constructive ways to control the stress that comes our way and to help our clients do the same. The bottom line is that either you control your stress or stress controls you. Pay attention to what your body, mind, and spirit need in order to reduce and manage stress. This includes a combination of physical activity, good nutrition, adequate rest and relaxation, contact with friends and loved ones, and some quiet time to engage in self-reflection.

How stress affects us has a lot to do with how we perceive reality and interpret events. Cognitive behavior therapy teaches us that our thinking greatly influences how we feel and how we act. Specific cognitive behavior strategies can assist us in modifying our self-defeating beliefs. My students who have practiced changing their faulty thinking by applying cognitive techniques have attested to the value of critically evaluating their beliefs. When they have effectively modified some negative and unrealistic beliefs, these students feel more in control of their life. Cognitive restructuring helps us become more aware of our faulty thinking, which enables us to change these patterns. We can learn the difference between those aspects of reality that we can control and those that we cannot, and we can choose how we interpret and respond to our situation. One useful approach to managing stress is by learning to identify, critically evaluate, and ultimately change our faulty beliefs.

Cognitive behavior techniques have helped me understand that some of my stress is largely generated by the way I process events in life. I can recall looking out at an audience and seeing what I perceived to be a disapproving face. If there were 100 attendees in the audience, I would invariably find the one or two disapproving faces and ask myself, "Why don't they like the ideas I am presenting, and even more important, why don't they like me?" The principles of cognitive therapy were helpful to me in critically examining my faulty expectation of universal approval, which can lead to disappointment and self-criticism. I would like to think that I am impervious to the evaluation of others, but negative comments on evaluations from a conference presentation or from my classes still sting and can be mildly stressful. I recognize the impact of criticism on my performance, and I continue to work at not clinging to negative evaluations. I have learned that modifying self-defeating thinking and self-talk is an ongoing process.

If you don't take care of your body, where will you live?

This is a serious message. I devote considerable time to taking care of my body, and I plan some physical activity every day. I enjoy walking and hiking, but I am too attached to the comforts of home to sleep on the ground in the forest. However, I can walk on a mountain path for several hours and enjoy the journey, and I like my frequent bike rides in nature. Not only am I taking care of my body, I am also keeping psychologically fit. My exercise program may be partly responsible for maintaining my weight. I can still fit into the wedding suit I wore 55 years ago. If that suit were still in style, I would be wearing it today!

I participate in Pilates lessons and group classes several times a week even though I grunt and groan and often exclaim that I am too old for this stuff. Pilates is physically exerting, and I cannot say I am fond of this challenge, but I recognize its clear advantages for my overall health and physical balance. I feel better physically by increasing my physical strength, flexibility, and body awareness. This has made me more aware of my posture and has prevented me from losing my balance and falling a number of times. I am the only man in the class, and the women tease me when I cannot keep up. One of my Pilates instructors was a student of mine in a theories of counseling class in the early 1980s, and she recalls how demanding that course was. Now the roles are reversed, and when I complain about how hard she pushes me, she says, "I learned how to challenge clients from you!" At a Christmas party in 2012, I received a coffee cup inscribed "Joseph Pilates Award for 2012." I drink from that cup often and am proud of that award.

Some of my friends and family say I am an exercise addict. Perhaps this is true, but I see my physical activity as a positive addiction. For the past few years, I have engaged in about 18 hours of physical exercise a week. Although it takes self-discipline, the rewards are worth the effort I devote to keeping fit through a consistent exercise program. I realize that most of you will not have this much time (and perhaps interest) to devote to physical exercise. Taking care of yourself by engaging in regular physical activity does not have to consume a great deal of time, so choose activities that you find enjoyable and reap the benefits of getting up and moving.

When we travel, I find ways to continue my exercise activities. Last year, Marianne and I went on a river cruise along the Danube River. If the ship did not dock during the day, I walked around the ship many times. Perhaps some folks thought I was strange and wondered what I was doing walking in circles. Eventually, one older person got out of his chair and started walking behind me, and soon after another person joined us. Before long eight people were walking behind me like ducklings, and they seemed to like moving! Designing a plan to keep in physical and psychological shape is an individual matter. Keeping physically fit can be invigorating and relaxing as well as being a way to cope with the stress of daily life.

How do diet and nutrition play a key role in physical and mental health?

Our daily diet affects our long-term health more than any other factor within our control. Within the limits set by genetics, the foods we choose have a lot to do with our health. Irregular and inconsistent eating patterns are a key nutritional problem for many. I often hear students say they do not have time to eat. It is difficult to develop sound diet and nutrition practices when the consequences of not doing so may not be immediate. Learning how to eat wisely and well is an important step in a lifelong process toward wellness. By establishing healthy eating habits, we increase our ability to maintain the vitality that is necessary for us to provide quality care to our clients.

I do not skimp when it comes to eating regular meals. Developing regular and consistent eating patterns and establishing a healthy nutritional plan have given me the energy to meet the demands of everyday life. It can be useful to monitor what and how much you eat. I have recorded my eating patterns from time to time to increase my awareness of when and what I eat.

Set yourself up for success rather than failure, and be kind to yourself when you fall short in attending to your physical and psychological well-being. Making healthy choices about diet and nutrition entails having specific knowledge about the foods we eat; we must all become smart nutrition consumers. It is easy to feel overwhelmed by all the information available today about diet and nutrition, but it is critical for us to choose how we will nourish our body. I am pretty sure that nothing I have said here about diet and nutrition is new. The problem is putting what we know about good nutrition and diet into action and making life-enhancing decisions. Bon appétit!

For further reading on diet and nutrition, I highly recommend *Lean and Fit: A Doctor's Journey to Healthy Nutrition and Greater Wellness* (Scherger, 2019).

Reflection Questions

1. Do you agree that self-care is an ethical mandate and not a luxury? Why or why not?
2. How satisfied are you with your own self-care practices? In what areas would you want to make changes? How ready are you to make a commitment to taking actions leading to the changes you want?
3. How resilient do you see yourself as being? What specific things can you do to become more resilient?
4. If you were to create a self-care action plan, what would it look like?
5. What are your thoughts about the best way to prevent burnout? How willing are you to make use of strategies to prevent burnout in your life?

Chapter 9

Theorizing About Theories

Introduction

A theory is a general framework that enables you to make sense of the many facets of the counseling process. It provides a perspective that gives direction to what you do and say. Developing this perspective takes a great deal of time, personal reflection, and supervised clinical experience. Your theory needs to be appropriate for your client population, setting, and the type of counseling you provide. At best, a theory becomes an integral part of the person you are and is an expression of your uniqueness.

In this chapter, I explain how I have developed my own theoretical orientation over many years. I describe the theories I am particularly drawn to and why I think a theory is essential for effective counseling practice. I share my bias toward an integrative approach to counseling because I believe it is the most relevant route to pursue in meeting the diverse needs of our clientele.

• • •

How did you choose a theory as your foundation for counseling?

When I began my doctoral program in counseling in 1962, I took two courses devoted to "counseling procedures," but I had no comprehensive course on theories of counseling. We were taught only two major approaches to counseling: directive and nondirective approaches. I had to do extensive reading in the various theories of counseling after graduating from a doctoral program to learn more about contemporary theories. I made the greatest strides in identifying and developing my theoretical orientation when I began teaching a course in the theories of counseling in 1973. As I taught my students about the various theories, I became convinced that each of the theoretical models had something unique to offer.

My interest in existential psychology and psychotherapy, which began in graduate school, has developed into the foundation of my theory. What initially drew me toward this approach is its emphasis on choice, freedom, responsibility, and self-determination. During my adolescent and early adulthood years, I did not trust that I could be the author of my life. Freedom of choice was associated with anxiety, which I wanted to avoid. Instead of looking inward and accepting responsibility for making choices in my life, I looked to external authorities to tell me how to live. My personal journey has shown me how basic the key existential themes are in understanding myself.

Existential notions that I find especially valuable, both personally and professionally, include the following: meaning in life is not static, we constantly re-create ourselves through our projects; anxiety goes along with the freedom to choose our way and needs to be explored, not eliminated; and we are mortal beings, and that fact serves as a wake-up call to take stock of how we are living. Facing the inevitable prospect of death gives the present moment significance; we become aware that we do not have forever to accomplish our goals. The reality of death is a catalyst that can challenge us to create a life that has meaning and purpose. Existential therapy is not so much a complete theory as it is a way of viewing and understanding the psychotherapy venture. I operate on its assumption that we are the architects of our own lives. If we don't like the design of our present existence, we can take steps to revise the blueprints. Counseling is a journey in which the therapist is a guide who facilitates a client's exploration in a life-changing process.

How did your quest to define your personal theoretical orientation to counseling develop?

Existential therapy has become the foundation of my integrative approach to counseling, but the existential approach is not infused with techniques. I believe the crucial factor in a healing relationship revolves around who the therapist is as a person rather than the techniques that are used. My main interests are in being as fully present as I can be with my client, establishing a trusting relationship, creating safety, and understanding the client's subjective world. If my client is able to sense my presence and my desire to make a real connection, then a solid foundation is being created for our work together. The client-therapist relationship is of the utmost importance because the quality of this relationship offers a context for change, and it is the therapeutic relationship that heals emotional wounds. Although I incorporate techniques from various therapeutic models, especially the cognitive behavior therapy (CBT) and Gestalt therapy, these interventions are made within the context of striving to understand the subjective world of the client.

A feature I particularly value in all the cognitive behavior therapies (CBTs) is the demystification of the therapy process. Clients are active, informed, and responsible for the direction of therapy. These therapies are all based on an educational model and emphasize the therapeutic alliance between therapist and client, which makes CBT a good fit with the existential approach. Cognitive behavior therapists encourage self-help, seek continuous feedback from the client on how well treatment strategies are working, and provide a structure and direction to the therapy process that allows for the evaluation of outcomes. Typically, a therapist educates clients about the nature and course of their problem, the process of cognitive therapy, and how thoughts influence emotions and behaviors.

I am also very much drawn to Gestalt therapy, which is based on existential premises. Gestalt methods bring conflicts and human struggles to life. Gestalt therapy is a creative approach that uses experiments to move clients from talk to action and experience. Techniques in CBT are typically introduced to bring about some action or elicit some emotion or to achieve a goal, whereas experiments grow out of the interaction between client and therapist and emerge within what is taking place in the present moment. For example, a client who speaks in a very soft voice can be asked to experiment with increasing the volume to see what she experiences when she speaks louder. A client who tends to asks many questions as a way of communicating could be asked to make direct statements. The therapist might ask a client who goes into great detail in talking about a personal concern to experiment with giving his key message in one sentence. All of these experiments give clients a chance to try on new behavior and observe how this is different from a familiar behavior. The creative and spontaneous use of active experiments is a pathway to experiential learning.

How has your theoretical orientation evolved over the course of your career?

One way that my theoretical orientation has evolved over the course of my career is my increased awareness of the role cultural diversity plays in effective counseling practice. In the early 1960s, little attention was given to diversity and multicultural perspectives. Over the years I began to see how all interventions are multicultural and how crucial it is to understand the complex role that diversity and similarity play in our theoretical orientation to counseling practice. Through my continuing education efforts and dialogues with colleagues who were pioneers in the field of multicultural counseling, I eventually realized that clients and counselors bring a variety of attitudes, values, culturally learned assumptions, biases, beliefs, and behaviors to the therapeutic relationship. From both an ethical and a clinical perspective, I began writing about how our practices need to be accurate, appropriate, and meaningful for the clients with whom we work. We needed to rethink our theories and modify our techniques to meet our clients' unique needs rather than applying interventions in the same manner to all clients.

For further reading on my journey and how I developed my theoretical orientations, see *Theory and Practice of Counseling and Psychotherapy* (Corey, 2021) and *The Art of Integrative Counseling* (Corey, 2019). An excellent resource on meaning in life and how this can be integrated into many theoretical approaches is *Meaning in Life: A Therapist's Guide* (Hill, 2018).

If you had to pick three theorists that have significantly influenced your thinking about counseling theories, who would they be? How have they influenced your view of counseling practice?

It is not easy to limit myself to three key theorists because many have been influential in my work, but three people who have influenced my thinking would definitely include Alfred Adler, Carl Rogers, and Albert Ellis. What these theorists have in common is that each was a rebel in his own way. They did not accept the status quo, and they courageously put forth their own vision of how therapy could best lead to a life-changing process. I have not been a devotee of any one theory, instead borrowing ideas that resonate with me from various theorists. I have done my best to be creative and forge my own path, and these theorists have been role models for me, taking active steps in looking at how to bring about constructive change. I have written a chapter on each of these pioneering theorists in several of my counseling theories books, but here I will highlight how their life experiences shaped their view of counseling theory and practice. I also discuss a few of their major contributions to the field, and how their work influenced my theoretical perspective.

Alfred Adler, a contemporary of Sigmund Freud, was a forerunner of the humanistic movement in psychology. Adler's early childhood was not a happy time; his experiences were characterized by a struggle to overcome weaknesses and feelings of inferiority, and the basic concepts of his theory grew out of his willingness to deal with his personal problems. He is an example of a person who shaped his own life as opposed to having it determined by fate. Adler was a poor student, yet with determined effort he eventually excelled in school. He went on to study medicine at the University of Vienna, specialized in neurology and psychiatry, and he had a keen interest in incurable childhood diseases.

Adler had the courage to challenge what he believed to be the limitations of Freud's psychoanalytic theory. When we realize that Adler was on the scene about 100 years ago, his visionary ideas were truly remarkable. Adler had a passionate concern for the common person and was outspoken about child-rearing practices, school reforms, and prejudices that resulted in conflict. He advocated for children at risk, women's rights, the equality of the sexes, adult education, community mental health, family counseling, and brief therapy. Adler created 32 child guidance clinics in the Vienna public schools and began training teachers, social workers, physicians, and other professionals. He pioneered the practice of teaching professionals through live demonstrations with parents and children before large audiences. Adler exhibited courage in doing more than simply writing and lecturing about his theory; he was willing to put his theory into practice through his live demonstrations.

Adler had an overcrowded work schedule most of his professional life, yet he still took some time to sing, enjoy music, and be with friends. Adler ignored the urging of his friends to slow down, and at age 67, while taking a walk before a scheduled lecture in Aberdeen, Scotland, he collapsed and died of heart failure. Indeed, he died way too young, but in his lifetime he made major contributions that are still influencing contemporary practice.

As I read about Adler's life, I see many parallels to my own life in the personal issues he faced and how he dealt with these themes. Like Adler, I was unhappy and lonely during my early childhood. I was a poor student in grade school, and as noted previously, I even failed fifth grade. I knew well the feelings of inferiority, and I found ways to compensate for my inferiority. Like Adler, I have experienced a very crowded work schedule since the beginning of my career. My friends have often encouraged me to slow down and smell the roses! Perhaps my fondness toward Adler as a person and his theory rest in the ways my journey resonates with his path.

Many of the Adlerian concepts have significantly influenced my perspective on what counseling is about. Let me select just a few of Adler's ideas that I have incorporated into my integrative theory of counseling. I think our past plays a key role in the person we are today. I like that Adler emphasized the value of learning about past experiences, yet at the same time offered hope for us to change our present life. The emphasis on recollecting early memories is fascinating, and I frequently use early recollections in working with clients and members of my groups. My group work practice has been influenced by several Adlerian concepts, including an emphasis on the social forces that motivate behavior, finding meaning and purpose in life, and the search for mastery as a way of overcoming inferiority. The patterns that people develop out of their relationships with their parents and siblings and the notion that we create a unique style of life as a response to our perceived inferiority keenly interest me.

Carl Rogers, a major figure in the development of humanistic psychology, founded what is known as the person-centered approach. In my mind, he is one of the most influential figures in revolutionizing the direction of counseling theory and practice. He emphasized the importance of nonjudgmental listening and acceptance as a condition for people to feel free enough to change. A central concept of Rogers's theory pertains to the value of autonomy, which seems to have grown out of his own struggles to become independent from his parents. Rogers grew up in a home where strict religious standards governed behavior. In his early years, while at a seminary studying to be a minister, Rogers made a critical choice that influenced his personal life and the focus of his theory. As a college student, he realized that he could no longer go along with the religious thinking of his parents, which led to his psychological independence. He took the risk of writing a letter to his parents telling them that his views were changing from fundamentalist to liberal and that he was developing his own philosophy of life. He showed a questioning stance toward life, a genuine openness to change, and demonstrated the courage to pursue unknown paths in both his personal and professional lives. As is true for Adler, I suspect that I am drawn to Rogers as a person and a professional because I see ways that I have struggled to achieve a sense of personal autonomy. Like Rogers, I modified some of my religious and life values and dared to disagree with some of the teachings that I experienced. When I ask students to select a theory that comes closest to their personal belief system and is congruent with their life experiences, many of my students tell me that they are drawn to those theorists with whom they share some similar life struggles.

Rogers was not afraid to take a strong position, and he challenged the status quo throughout his professional career. He has been called a "quiet revolutionary," a personality trait that I greatly appreciate. During the last 15 years of his life, Rogers applied the person-centered approach to world peace by training policymakers, leaders, and groups in conflict. One of his greatest passions was directed toward the reduction of interracial tensions and the effort to achieve world peace, for which he was nominated for the Nobel Peace Prize.

The person-centered approach to therapy rests on the core therapeutic conditions of empathy, unconditional positive regard, and therapist genuineness. Rogers's view of these therapeutic factors resonates with me, and I am convinced that they are necessary, but not sufficient, factors to facilitate change in individuals. The work that Rogers did on the therapeutic relationship is of paramount importance. In my teaching, I tell students that it is the quality of the relationship they establish with clients that makes change possible. There is abundant research supporting the role of the therapeutic relationship. I believe that a strong working alliance, or therapeutic relationship, needs to be the foundation of any theory. It is not the theory we hold, nor the techniques we use, that heal clients, instead it is the relationship that heals. I appreciate the contributions Rogers made, and I have incorporated them into my integrative theory.

Albert Ellis is truly a pioneer who has earned the right to be known as the father of rational emotive behavior therapy (REBT) and the grandfather of cognitive behavior therapy. Ellis developed active-directive ways of working with people in his clinical practice. At professional conferences, I have seen Albert Ellis and Carl Rogers engaged in debates about how therapy is best done. Ellis was fond of saying he agreed with Rogers on the importance of providing clients with unconditional positive regard, but he challenged Rogers on most of his other theoretical positions. Ellis loudly disagreed with Rogers's passive and nondirective stance and was convinced people needed forceful techniques to change their irrational thinking. Ellis was without doubt a rebel who was willing to challenge what he believed to be ineffective ways of doing therapy. From him I learned the value of identifying beliefs that are faulty and taking an active stance in disputing irrational beliefs and replacing them with constructive beliefs. I have incorporated the emphasis on examining how my thinking is instrumental in the way I feel and how I act. Ellis's works have convinced me that if we hope to modify the way we experience and express emotions, we must explore our belief systems. If we want to change certain behaviors, it is useful to assess the way our thinking is linked to our behavior. Ellis created a number of techniques I have incorporated in assisting clients in replacing ineffective beliefs with constructive cognitions.

Ellis greatly enjoyed his work and teaching REBT, which was his passion and primary commitment in life. I appreciate Ellis's dedication to his work and can identify with being very involved in continuing my life's work. Ellis gave workshops wherever he went in his travels, and he often said, "I wouldn't go to the Taj Mahal unless they asked me to do a workshop there!"

Ellis had many physical challenges for most of his life, yet he lived an active and very productive life until his death at age 93. I have incorporated many of the concepts and techniques Ellis taught and wrote about into my integrative approach to therapy, and in my personal life as well. I do not copy his confrontational and highly directive style, but I have found ways to implement his ideas in my therapeutic style.

How can I figure out which theoretical approach best suits me?

Whether you are a counselor-in-training or a new counseling professional, it is a good idea to familiarize yourself with what the various theoretical orientations have to offer. Functioning exclusively within the framework of one theory may not provide you with the therapeutic flexibility you need to deal creatively with the unique needs of diverse client populations. Even if you decide to work within the framework of a single theory, you will still need to adapt your approach and techniques to each client's needs. In many ways, your challenge will be to customize your theoretical perspective to each individual with whom you work. You are creating a new therapy for each client!

Regardless of your theoretical approach, you must decide *what* techniques, procedures, or intervention methods to utilize, *when* to use them, and with *which* clients. For counseling to be effective, techniques and procedures must be consistent with your client's values, worldview, life experiences, and cultural background. Avoid using techniques in a rigid way; these are merely tools to assist you in effectively reaching your clients. Personalize your techniques so they fit your style and the needs of your clients, and invite clients to give you feedback about how well your techniques are working for them.

All counseling theories have both unique contributions and limitations. It is useful to study many contemporary theories to determine which concepts and techniques you will most want to incorporate into your approach to practice. All theoretical approaches have something of value to offer, so students and practitioners do well to remain open to thinking from an integrative perspective. No single theory is comprehensive enough to account for the complexities of human behavior when the full range of client types and their specific problems are considered. This is why I encourage my students to avoid becoming a devotee to any one theory. Most counselors today are leaning toward integration of several theories.

It is wise to search for an approach that fits who you are as a person and to think about your client population and the setting in which you work. I draw from an interactive thinking, feeling, and behaving model because a complete therapeutic approach needs to address all aspects of human functioning. I attend to what clients most need at a particular moment in a session. I attempt to address what clients are thinking, how their thinking affects how they feel, and what they are doing. Paying attention to what clients are experiencing provides clues to which dimension is the most salient to explore. This kind of integration implies that you have a basic knowledge of various theoretical systems and counseling techniques.

What are some ways I can develop an integrative approach to counseling?

Integrative approaches attempt to tailor both the techniques used and the relationship style to the needs of individual clients. Developing an integrative perspective requires having a good conceptual grasp of a number of theories, being open to the idea that these theories can be integrated in some ways, and being willing to test your hypotheses to determine how well they are working. Study many of the contemporary theories to determine which concepts and techniques you want to incorporate into your approach to practice. A basic knowledge of various theoretical systems and counseling techniques is required to work effectively with diverse client populations in various settings.

If you are a new counseling professional, I suggest selecting the primary theory closest to your basic beliefs. Learn this theory in as much depth as possible, yet at the same time be open to examining other theories. By working within the framework of a primary theory, you will have an anchor point from which to construct your own counseling perspective. Be willing to be flexible in the way in which you apply the techniques that flow from a primary theory as you work with different clients.

If you are currently a counselor-in-training, it is not realistic to expect that you will already have an integrated and well-defined theoretical model. With time and reflective study, you can develop a consistent conceptual framework and choose from among the many techniques you have learned. Developing your personalized approach is a lifelong endeavor that will be refined with clinical experience, reading, reflection, and engagement with colleagues. The challenge for you is to think and practice in an integrative manner intentionally and critically. Be open to supervision throughout your career. Talk with supervisors and colleagues about what you are doing. Discuss some of your interventions with other professionals, and think of alternative approaches you could take with clients. Continue reflecting on what fits for you and what set of blueprints is most useful in creating your emerging model for practice.

An integrative approach rests on the foundation of a systematic rationale for what you actually do in your work. Avoid merely picking and choosing concepts and techniques without a rationale. At its best, integration is a creative synthesis of the unique contributions of diverse approaches, dynamically integrating concepts and techniques that fit the uniqueness of your personality and style.

I predict that future integrative counseling perspectives will find common ground that unites the diverse range of single theories. We may not have a universal theory yet, but efforts will continue to combine the best elements of the various theoretical approaches and work toward an integrated theory.

Some books I recommend for further reading on integrative approaches to counseling are the *Handbook of Psychotherapy Integration* (Norcross & Goldfried, 2019) and *The Art of Integrative Counseling* (Corey, 2019).

Reflection Questions

1. What one theory comes closest to being congruent with your values and view of counseling?
2. What personal qualities or characteristics may help you identify with a specific theory when exploring an integrative approach? How might these qualities help you in synthesizing your integrative approach?
3. To what extent does an integrative approach to counseling practice appeal to you? How can you best develop your own approach to counseling?
4. How do you determine whether an intervention you are planning to use is suitable for a client? How can you use feedback from your clients to modify your interventions with them?
5. If you were applying for an internship placement and were asked to describe your theory of counseling, what would your answer be?

Chapter 10

The Practice of
Group Counseling

Introduction

Group work has increased in popularity over the past couple of decades. Many counselors recognize that group work can be as effective and, in some cases, even more effective than individual counseling. Group members not only gain insights and increased self-awareness but have opportunities to practice new skills both within the group and in their everyday interactions outside the group. Group members can learn how to cope with their problems by observing and interacting with others who have similar life situations. Members of the group benefit from the feedback of other group members as well as feedback from the leader. If the group membership is diverse with respect to age, interests, background, socioeconomic status, and type of problem, the group represents a microcosm of society. The diversity that characterizes most groups helps participants see themselves through the eyes of a wide range of people.

In a supportive and safe atmosphere, members can experiment with new behaviors. As they practice these behaviors in the group, members receive reinforcement and learn how to translate their new insights into action in daily life. The group experience serves as a living laboratory; it becomes a mirror in which members see themselves as they are and in which they can acquire new skills for more effective interpersonal relating. Groups provide a sense of community, which can be an antidote to the impersonal world in which participants may live.

This chapter addresses many of the questions I have been asked about group work. I am passionate about the benefits of group counseling and encourage counseling students to participate in various kinds of groups for their personal and professional development. I hope this discussion stimulates your interest in reading more about the benefits of group counseling.

• • •

How can I best screen and select members for a group?

My graduate program had almost no coursework in group counseling and no training in this area. During my doctoral program and in my early career, I participated in many different workshops and groups. Although the quality of these groups varied, as a member I learned some valuable lessons about what makes a group effective. In some cases, I learned what I did not want to do as a group counselor.

When I began my work as a group counselor in the 1960s, many groups were put together with very little attention to screening, selecting, and preparing individuals for a group experience. I have organized and conducted many therapeutic groups for about 60 years, and I am convinced that group members will become more engaged and derive the maximum benefit if they have adequate preparation for the group experience. I am a firm supporter of the value of making the effort to screen, select, and prepare members for any group I offer. I want potential members to know what the group is about so they can determine whether this group is what they want and need. Most of the groups I have offered have been counseling groups and other kinds of therapeutic groups, and it is essential to meet privately with every person who wishes to join the group. During this meeting, I get a sense of the appropriateness of including particular candidates and give them a chance to determine whether they want to be involved in the group. This interview is a two-way exchange, and a mutual decision will be made. I want individuals I am considering for a group to also interview me. I invite them to ask questions and get information from me that will enable them to make an informed choice about joining a group.

How is informed consent handled in group work?

In the 1960s and 1970s, informed consent for groups was not a standard practice, and most of the groups I attended lacked any semblance of informed consent or information about what I could expect from the leader or the group. This convinced me that there should be no surprises for the participants, and I pay special attention to the informed consent process in my groups. I view the process of informed consent as a way to educate participants about how they can assume responsibility to accomplish their personal goals and how they can get the most from a group experience.

Informed consent is considered standard ethical and legal practice in group work today. Basic information about the group should be provided to potential group participants to assist them in deciding whether to enter the group and how to participate in it to maximize their learning. This information typically includes group leader qualifications, techniques that may be used, the nature and limitations of confidentiality, and the risks and benefits of participating in the group. Various aspects of the consent process may need to be revisited at different phases of a group. If members have adequate information, there is a greater chance that they will assume a collaborative role with the leader and will become actively engaged in the group.

For a more complete discussion of informed consent in groups, see *Groups: Process and Practice* (Corey, Corey, & Corey, 2018).

What drew you to group work? Why have you specialized in the field of group counseling?

When I was in my 30s and 40s I participated in many different groups, including overnight marathons, traditional weekly therapy groups, and a variety of residential personal growth workshops and encounter groups (ranging in length from a weekend to 10 days). For several years, I attended a number of marathon groups. These intense experiences enabled me to integrate my emotional states with cognition. It was difficult for me to identify and express a range of emotions in my personal therapy, and sessions often became an intellectual exercise with me trying to figure out my dynamics! In contrast, as a group member I became emotionally engaged, not only in my own work but also through interactions with others in the group. I found intensive group experiences to be more useful for me than individual therapy, and I participated in a variety of therapeutic group experiences.

I learned the value of a sustained format that creates a sense of community and fosters intensity. These experiences also filled a gap in my graduate training, providing practical lessons in group process both as a member and as a facilitator. I also received additional indirect benefits I could apply to my professional work, especially in my initial efforts to create a variety of groups at the university counseling center where I worked as a counselor. From my own experiences as a group member, I learned important lessons about what I wanted to do or not do as a group practitioner.

I consider groups to be the treatment of choice for many client populations. Groups provide a natural laboratory and a sense of community that demonstrate to people that they are not alone with their problems and that there is hope for making changes and creating a better life. Designing and facilitating groups for many years has demonstrated to me that groups can be highly effective, offer unique opportunities for new learning, and have the power to move people in creative and more life-enhancing directions.

Do you have any suggestions for how to work best with a coleader in a group?

There are many advantages to a coleadership format, for both the group itself and for the coleaders, and I prefer to work with a coleader. Selecting a coleader involves effort, and getting a group launched is a team effort. Coleaders should meet both before and after each group session to assess what is going on in the group, to talk about how they are working together as a team, and to make tentative plans for future sessions. This is fundamental to the success of the group. These meetings are well worth the time spent thinking about the group and how to best facilitate the themes that are emerging.

It is important for coleaders to have mutual respect for each other. Although coleaders may not have the same style of leadership, it is important that they share a similar philosophy regarding how groups can best function to be of value to the members. When I am cofacilitating a session, we do not take turns or decide in advance who will open a session and who will close it. We are spontaneous and bring ourselves freely into the work taking place, and we typically interact with each other during the group session.

If a conflict occurs between coleaders, how can this best be managed?

There have been times when a coleader and I had a difference of opinion regarding how to proceed. Working with many different coleaders over many years, I know that coleaders can skillfully model healthy conflict resolution for group members. Modeling nondefensiveness and a willingness to challenge and be challenged by one another can be a valuable learning opportunity. It can be a healing experience for group members to see the coleaders address a conflict in an effective manner. However, a conflict or confrontation that is poorly handled places an unfair burden on the members and can be harmful to the cohesion within a group. Coleaders need to determine whether an issue is best addressed in private or in the moment with the group members. If the members witnessed the conflict, my inclination is to address it in the group. If the conflict is resolved by meeting privately, the coleaders need to share with the members how the conflict was resolved. Not doing so results in the group members being left to wonder what happened.

Years ago I was a member in a weekend group cofacilitated by a couple who were in an intimate relationship. They brought their relationship struggles as a couple in their personal life into the group. The time and energy they devoted to attempting to resolve long-standing conflicts and tensions as a couple detracted from the members having the time they deserved to address the concerns they came to the group to explore. Coleaders who have an intimate relationship with each other need to be mindful that their leadership role is to facilitate group interaction among members, not to use the group for their own therapy.

As a group facilitator, how can I create trust within a group at an early stage?

The kind of person you are and your ability to establish connections with others are likely to be the major determinants of the level of trust in your groups. The therapeutic relationship is best established by paying attention to the needs of individual members, responding to them in respectful ways, demonstrating interest in them, appropriately self-disclosing, stating your expectations openly, being sensitive to the fears and anxieties of the members, and providing group members with opportunities to openly say what they are feeling or thinking.

I have been able to apply many of the lessons I learned by being a member of a group to being a group leader. Being encouraged to talk about our fears and hesitations as well as our hopes and expectations about being in the group helped me. During the initial stage of a group, members are getting acquainted, learning how the group functions, learning the norms that will govern group behavior, exploring their fears and hopes pertaining to the group, clarifying their expectations, identifying personal goals, and determining whether this group is a safe place for them to be open about their concerns. I directly address the matter of trust and safety at the first meeting. I ask participants what it will take for them to willingly be vulnerable and to take risks. I encourage members to identify any anxieties and concerns they have about being in the group and to begin talking about these concerns. This is a good way to demonstrate to members that their concerns are being taken seriously. Unexpressed anxieties tend to get in the way of members sharing deeper parts of themselves. I consistently tell members that trust is not something that just happens; rather, it is the outcome of their willingness to talk about what they are experiencing here and now in the group.

Sometimes members want to give me more credit than I deserve for creating trust in a group that in many ways resembles a loving family. I have a part in contributing to a safe setting, but I want members to recognize what they did to foster trust and cohesion in their group. I want them to take full credit for establishing a therapeutic and supportive atmosphere. If they can do this, there is a good chance that they can translate what they learned in the group to creating more positive relationships in daily life.

How can cultural factors contribute to reluctance on the part of group members?

Some members may have difficulty being direct because their culture values a less direct style of communication. Even if I prize being direct, it is not my place to insist that members embrace my view of desirable styles of communication. As a group leader, I can minimize reluctance on the part of members by encouraging a discussion of how they could participate in the group in a way that does not violate their cultural norms and values. As I become increasingly aware of the cultural context of the members of a group, it is possible to both appreciate their cultural values and respectfully encourage them to deal with their personal concerns. One of my functions is to assist members in understanding how their initial hesitation to reveal themselves may relate to their cultural background.

Some techniques I introduce in a group are aimed at assisting members in expressing their feelings, but certain members may find this offensive. Some members may be very slow to express emotions openly or to talk freely about problems within their family. They may have been taught to withhold their feelings and that it is improper to display emotional reactions publicly. Other members may experience difficulty asking for time in the group because they have learned that to do so is selfish, insensitive, and self-oriented. Rather than telling these members to speak up or to rely on them to initiate self-disclosure, I sometimes ask them to consider sharing at least one reaction they had as they listened to a particular member speak. By providing some structure, I am able to encourage members to express themselves in a less threatening way. It is important to understand the role society has played in oppressing some members into silence. Social factors and cultural norms shed a different light on the reluctance of group members to engage in self-disclosure and to verbally participate in the group. Group cohesion can be increased by inviting all members to become active participants in their own ways.

Do you ever see it as your role to help educate group members about multicultural issues? If so, how do you approach this?

I have had the privilege of presenting workshops in several countries and with different cultural groups. Interacting with people from other cultures has taught me a great deal about approaching people with whom we work with an open mind and an open heart. In each of these cultural experiences, I learned how important it is to put my personal agenda aside and work with any differences I encounter in an individual or a group in a respectful way. I continue to be reminded that my way of thinking is not suitable for everyone I meet.

As a microcosm of society, groups provide a context for addressing issues of power, privilege, discrimination, social injustice, and oppression. As these themes emerge in a group, I think it is my responsibility to help members openly explore them. I don't see it as my role to directly teach, but I try to facilitate a process that invites members to educate one another about their culture and how their culture affects them. I certainly see opportunities for all of the participants to learn about multicultural issues in a diverse group, and I do my best to become aware of my own assumptions about differences and to check any biases that I hold.

By adopting an open stance of being interested in how cultural factors are operating in the lives of group members, many opportunities arise for members to learn from each other. For example, I recall a person of color in one of our groups describing how he was frequently stopped by police while driving his car, but he was never charged with any offense. He wanted to express his anger, pain, and fear and talk about the impact discrimination had on him. It was also an opportunity for him to talk to others in the group about being unfairly treated based on his race. Other group members were able to learn how discrimination is harmful and how it can have an enduring impact. This member's personal account of being discriminated against carried a powerful message and resulted in a deeper understanding by all group members.

When leading court-ordered and mandated involuntary groups, how can we increase the chances that members will have a positive experience?

Too often it is assumed that not much will occur in involuntary groups because members are forced to attend, but I do not agree with this assumption. I have worked with involuntary groups in training situations and with students in required group courses, and I am convinced that these groups can have positive outcomes if the leader attends to the unique factors of mandatory group participation. A good place to begin working with mandatory groups is by exploring the attitudes and reactions individuals bring with them and what they have been told about the group. It is likely that these individuals have very little accurate knowledge about how groups function or about what they might gain from participating. They are likely to have a cynical attitude and not see any value in participating. A key role for the leader is to clarify misconceptions about group work and to educate these members in how to use the group.

For many years, my colleagues and I conducted 4-day training workshops for the treatment staff at a state mental hospital. It was crucial to deal with attitudes the staff may have about being required to attend training sessions. A times, we encountered negative reactions from staff members who felt they were singled out for the training because they lacked skills as therapists. We invited them to talk about their feelings and found this was a good place to begin the workshops. Although many of them could be considered involuntary group participants at the beginning, if they were open to refining their skills or acquiring new skills, they acknowledged how valuable this workshop had been for them, both personally and professionally. By dealing with their initial resistance to participating in training, they also had a better appreciation for what many of their patients experience in the groups in the hospital.

I have taught group counseling courses for students in a master's degree program in counseling in an intensive weeklong format at various universities. These courses were perceived by some students to be just another requirement that they had to meet. These courses have both didactic and experiential aspects, and students spend some time in a group as a member. Some of the students in these group classes tested my patience and challenged my abilities as a group counselor educator. In spite of doing thorough advanced preparation so students knew what would be expected of them, a fair number of students refused to actively participate in the experiential aspects of the course. I attempted to facilitate a discussion around what was contributing to their reluctance to become engaged in personal ways in the group class. Some students could not understand the rationale for engaging in any kind of personal self-disclosure in their graduate program. Others were hesitant to share personal concerns because they did not want to be judged by their peers. Some claimed that they would have other classes with one another and would not know how to interact with each other in these classes. Exploring the fears and concerns of students often resulted in a positive change in attitudes and behaviors. Talking about the students' fears of being judged led to a shift within the group. Many of them were able to take the risk of being more open and shared some of their struggles in their personal life, as well as being in the group, which led to increased cohesion in the group. In several of these group classes, members came to the conclusion that they could be a support group for one another as they progressed through their graduate program.

When working with any kind of involuntary group, special attention must be given to teaching members about the potential value they can derive from the group. Educating members about the group process is critical, including clearly and fully informing involuntary members of the nature and goals of the group, procedures that will be used, the rights of members to decline certain activities, the limitations of confidentiality, and ways active participation in the group may affect their life outside the group. I certainly have expectations of involuntary members who join my groups, and I clearly present these expectations to the members. If they attend a group but do not participate, I inform them that this will be documented in their clinical file. I want to find out from the members who have been sent to my group what the consequences will be for them if they choose not to attend, and I encourage them to talk about their choices in a nonjudgmental way. I want the members to understand the consequences of lack of compliance with the group program and that I will not automatically certify that they have benefited from the group if they refused to take part. I do my best to assist involuntary members in making the transition to voluntary participation. I put forth considerable effort in creating a climate based on acceptance and respect in which involuntary members can recognize that there could be potential personal benefits from participating in this group.

How do you handle conflict that emerges in a group?

Conflict can be expected in all relationships, both in daily life and in groups. Conflicts that arise in the group need to be acknowledged, addressed, explored, and effectively managed. Conflict is typically a source of anxiety for both the group leader and members, and there is a tendency for the group to avoid conflict rather than spend the time and effort necessary to work through it. Unexplored conflict often leads to a hidden agenda and a general lack of trust in the group.

A group is an ideal place for participants to challenge their anxiety when conflict arises and learn how to directly deal with the sources of conflict. The manner in which conflict is dealt with will determine whether a group retreats or whether interactions among members deepen. Members are not likely to take risks or allow themselves to be vulnerable if they do not experience a sense of safety with the other members and the leaders. As uncomfortable as it may be, if members and leaders are willing to talk about what is going on, rather than attacking and judging one another, important lessons can be learned about conflict resolution. When conflict occurs in a group, there is value in staying with what is going on among members and leaders and working through conflicts in a constructive way.

When conflict occurs in a group, I tend to observe how members are interacting with one another before I intervene. I explore with members their observations about the conflict and frequently ask them to talk about what it is like for them to be in the group at that moment. The goal is to get members to focus on themselves and express how they are being affected by what is occurring in the group rather than attributing motives to the behavior of others. I make sure members state their observations in nonjudgmental ways and talk respectfully to others. I intervene by blocking members when they begin attacking each other, and I redirect them to focus on themselves. Although I cannot always prevent unkindness on the part of certain members, I take action to minimize the detrimental effects that may result from the conflict.

What is the value of members experiencing a catharsis in a group?

When I participated as a group member in some intensive groups, at times I experienced emotional breakthroughs that I found valuable. I tend to be somewhat cognitive, and experiencing a catharsis was personally meaningful to me. It gave me a perspective on the value of emotional work that can be part of a group. In a counseling or therapy group, participants often tap into emotional material that catches them by surprise. This frequently results in the release of intense emotions, such as crying, anger, emotional pain, sadness, guilt, or grief. When training group counselors, I found that these leaders often measured the success of a group by the degree of emotional intensity and the number of cathartic experiences members displayed. Although the expression of emotion is often a key component of the group process, catharsis itself is not the desired outcome. One member approached me during a break and said tearfully that she must not be getting anything from the group because she had not yet had a catharsis.

In the early years of facilitating weeklong therapeutic groups, my coleaders and I were impressed by the power of the pent-up feelings members released. We made the mistake of concluding that the catharsis a member experienced would necessarily lead to insight and action. Although it is often the case that cathartic experiences are healing, our follow-up group sessions showed us how important it is to explore the meaning associated with a catharsis. After members have expressed intense feelings, it is important to ask them to talk about what this release of feelings meant to them. Releasing feelings is not the end goal. Inviting members to connect their emotional releases with a cognitive perspective is what makes for a therapeutic outcome.

In meeting with the coleaders of these weeklong therapeutic groups over a long period of time, we learned that it is essential that we could answer these questions:

- Am I capable of handling the intensity of the catharsis or what might result from it?
- Is there enough time remaining in the group session to work with the emotions that arise to achieve some kind of resolution?
- Will I have subsequent sessions with the group member to deal with potential repercussions of the catharsis?
- Are my coleaders and I sensitive to the subtle line between facilitating catharsis for its therapeutic potential and invoking it for the sake of a dramatic effect?

Group therapists who lack training and experience may use powerful interventions to stir up emotions and open up problems that members have kept from full awareness, but these leaders may not know how to intervene with those who are experiencing a catharsis and fail to help members work through what they have experienced and bring some closure to it. Leaders must be able to be psychologically present as the member expresses emotions. If leaders are threatened by emotional intensity, they may distract members from experiencing and processing emotion. We need to be especially aware of times when we use techniques to evoke emotions to fulfill our own needs rather than those of the members.

For a more in-depth treatment on the value of catharsis and the appropriate use of techniques that stimulate emotional reactions, see *Group Techniques* (Corey, Corey, Callanan, & Russell, 2015).

Should members have the freedom to leave a group at any time they choose?

A leader's attitudes and policies about the freedom to leave a group should be explained at the initial group session and discussed as part of the informed consent process. In all of my groups, I tell the members that they are expected to attend all sessions and to inform me if they know they will miss a session or if they decide to stop attending the group. Although I do not want to subject members to a debate or to undue pressure to remain in a group, I do emphasize the serious impact that their leaving can have on the whole group and on themselves, especially if they leave without an explanation.

Participants can decide to leave a group for a variety of reasons, but I believe they have a responsibility to the therapist and the other group members to explain their reasons for wanting to leave. It can be harmful for members to leave without attending to what led up to them wanting to leave. It is also unfortunate for members to leave a group because of a misunderstanding about some feedback they may have received. It can be damaging to other members if they are left wondering if a person left the group because of something they said or did. If the member provides reasons for leaving to the group as a whole, other members have an opportunity to clarify their possible role in the person's decision to leave. If a member were to simply stop coming to the group without notification, I am likely to contact this person to explore the reasons for not attending. I have an ethical responsibility to do everything I can to protect individuals from harm due to their participation in a group.

How can the techniques used intensify work within a group?

I use a variety of approaches in facilitating what is unfolding in a group, and I provide members with a general understanding of the role of experiments and group techniques that I am using. The techniques I employ are often aimed at focusing members on how they can explore their concerns in the group. I don't use techniques to make things happen in a group because of my belief that something is always going on among the members.

My interventions typically arise spontaneously out of the work of the participants and are tailored to the evolving situation in a particular session. If members experience the group as being a safe place, they will be inclined to move into deeper work and to take risks. Students frequently ask what I would do if a person did not want to go along with a technique that I introduce. My style is to be invitational rather than confrontational, and I never force or pressure members to do something that does not seem right for them. Questions I raise are:

- "Would you be willing to try . . ."
- "I have an idea for an experiment you could carry out in the group. Would you be interested in . . ."
- "Do you want to go further with what you have just said?"
- "Would you try something on for size and see how it fits?"

In selecting techniques, I think about how to expand on a member's work or whatever is happening in the group. My aim is to build on what is transpiring within the group, and I adapt my interventions to fit the needs of group members. Timing is of the utmost importance in introducing strategies. If I do not respect individuals' boundaries and push beyond their readiness to change, this will be counterproductive and possibly harmful.

I make it a practice to follow the energy and the clues provided by the members rather than to be overly directive. By looking around the room, for example, I may notice that members show various signs of disengagement. A useful technique at such times is to encourage the members to express what they are aware of in the moment. I might say, "I notice that most of you are silent and are not responding to each other. I'd like to hear from each of you what is going on with you now." It is therapeutically useful to teach group participants how to assess what is occurring in the group process on an ongoing basis so they can become actively involved in determining the direction their group is taking. The quality of the relationship I have established with the members, and their relationship with one another, makes it possible to gauge the progress of the group and to judge the optimal time for inviting clients into areas they have previously avoided.

For a further elaboration on this topic, see *Group Techniques* (Corey, Corey, Callanan, & Russell, 2015).

What is the value of emphasizing a here-and-now focus in group counseling?

In my own work as a member in different therapy groups, I was asked by the group leader to avoid storytelling when I was talking about a problem situation. At times the leader would ask me to bring the person I was talking about symbolically into the room and talk to that person directly as though he or she was in the room with me. I found an amazing difference between talking about a problem and talking directly to this person. Bringing the person into the present symbolically got me emotionally engaged in my work. As a group member, I personally experienced the therapeutic power in working in the here and now.

I have carried this lesson about the power of a present-centered focus into my work as a group counselor. Members often go into detail when describing a problem situation and give reasons for what they are doing. My inclination is to invite members to move from talking about their concerns to bringing this to life by an enactment. When members bring up a present or past problem, or an anticipated situation, from outside of the group, I explore how this might be played out in the context of the present group. Students who have observed me doing live counseling demonstrations often notice a clear emphasis on the here and now and have asked about my rationale for this approach.

One example of a symbolic exploration in the here and now in a group is a scenario in our video, *Evolution of a Group*. One of the group members in the video, Casey, engages in role-play with my coleader, Marianne Corey (as her mother). Casey discloses that she is gay and expresses her sadness about having to keep her sexual orientation a secret from her mother. Casey had some fears that others might judge her, yet after exploring her fears, she found people to be very caring and accepting, which greatly increased her trust level. Casey agrees with Marianne's suggestion that it would be more meaningful to role-play with her mother in her native language (Vietnamese). Casey begins by revealing to her symbolic mother that she is gay. At some point Casey says, "I keep thinking what my mother would say back to me." Marianne asks Casey to reverse roles, "becoming her mother," and express what she imagines her mother would tell her about her disclosure. Casey says how meaningful and healing it was for her to speak to her mother directly in the here and now. We would not encourage Casey to say to her mother everything she expressed symbolically in this role-playing situation. It is up to Casey to decide if and when to open a dialogue with her mother. Even if Casey chooses not to approach her mother, her work in the group led to some important insights. Casey's mother may never be able to agree with Casey's decisions of how she wants to live her life, but Casey can come to an affirmation of herself as a person.

My experience with groups continues to teach me that the past, present, and future are all significant tenses, but the action is best played out in the present moment. The past is gone and the future has not yet arrived, but the present moment is alive with possibilities. Whether you are talking about something from your past or an anticipated future situation, I would consistently bring you into the here and now. There is power in the present.

If you see value in counseling clients from the perspective I have described, you are likely to find ways of using this approach with your clients. To engage clients in experiential role-playing scenarios in the here and now, it is useful to draw on your own experience. The best lessons in learning how to facilitate bringing members into the here and now are often based on what you have experienced in doing this in your own therapy.

For a demonstration of how to encourage members to bring their concerns into the here and now, see the video program *Groups in Action: Evolution and Challenges* (Corey, Corey, & Haynes, 2014).

What were some of the difficulties you experienced when you began doing group work?

The first hurdle associated with group work is the process of establishing a group and recruiting members. This is true in many settings, be it private practice, a school, or a community agency. When I worked in a university counseling center, some of my colleagues complained that they wanted to offer groups but that college students were either too busy to make a commitment to attend or did not see the value of participating in a group. To market groups and recruit college students, I made guest appearances in various psychology and health education classes on campus and gave talks on topics such as coping with stress, dealing with relationship problems, and using personal counseling as a resource for self-care. I told students what was available for them at the counseling center and described the various kinds of groups my colleagues and I were offering. Students seemed to appreciate my invitation to come to the counseling center; we eventually saw an increase in the number of students availing themselves of personal and educational counseling, and our groups began to fill.

A good way to begin designing a group was to conduct a needs survey on the university campus. Many students have been victims of violence, rape, sexual abuse, sexual harassment, racism, or discrimination. Groups that have the potential to address critical needs of students include career development and career planning groups, anxiety-management groups, stress-management groups, grief groups, cultural identity groups, nontraditional age student groups, groups for those with relationship concerns, groups dealing with body image, groups for survivors of trauma, self-esteem groups, groups for survivors of childhood sexual abuse, and personal identity groups. My experience in creating a variety of groups on the college campus showed me that effective group work is limited only by the needs of the population, the creativity of the counselor, and the effort it takes to promote the group. These groups provided a supportive climate in which students were able to acquire insights and skills in managing the personal and social dimensions of their lives. Group participation was effective in enabling students to deal with life transitions and challenges such as forming new relationships, coping with struggles pertaining to self-identity, and dealing with oppression. Doing group work on the campus convinced me that therapeutic and psychoeducational groups are a cost-effective way to meet the needs of a diverse range of college students. I also found facilitating these groups to be highly rewarding and worth the effort I had put into promoting them.

Reflection Questions

1. If you were considering joining a group, what would you want to know before making your decision?
2. What value and benefits do you see in group work?
3. What would you require to feel safe and trusting in a group?
4. If you were interested in establishing a group, what kind of group would you want to form?
5. What kind of coursework and training in group work have you had in your program? What have you thought about your education and training in group work?

Chapter 11

Becoming an Ethical Counselor

Introduction

Counselors are required to make ethical decisions from time to time as they work with clients, and counselors are responsible for the outcome of these decisions. When facing a challenging ethical decision, it is imperative to first consult with colleagues, supervisors, and experts. Even counselors with many years of field experience benefit from consultation with colleagues who can provide an important check on their thinking about the issue. You do not have to make these decisions alone, and I encourage you to reach out to others who can collaborate with you and help you think through all that is involved in practicing ethically.

You may believe you have resolved most of the ethical issues you might face in counseling practice, but as you develop experience as a counselor, these topics often take on new dimensions. Being an ethical practitioner is a developmental process that requires self-reflection, an open mind, consultation with other professionals, and continual reexamination. As you read the questions and answers in this chapter, reflect on what you think becoming an ethical counseling involves for you. To what extent do any of the answers provide a new perspective for you on what it means to strive toward ethical practice?

• • •

What is involved in becoming an ethical counseling practitioner?

Awareness of a standard of ethics is central to effective practice in counseling, but ethics codes provide only general standards. It is necessary for counselors to know and follow the legal dimensions of counseling practice, but complying with the law is not a sufficient standard for ethical practice. I urge students to go beyond thinking about avoiding a malpractice suit. It is important to recognize that the ethical decisions you make may change your life and the life of your client.

My students learn that many ethical dilemmas are complex and could have several excellent solutions. There is often no one best answer when it comes to responding to a situation involving ethics. Ethical dilemmas rarely have clear-cut answers, and you must acquire tolerance for dealing with gray areas and struggling with ambiguity. You are likely to encounter many situations in which the exercise of sound judgment is necessary to do the absolute best for your clients. Becoming an ethical practitioner requires that you use informed, sound, and responsible judgment.

How did you get interested in teaching ethics, and how do students approach taking your ethics in counseling course?

When I was in my doctoral program in counseling, we did not have a separate course on ethics. A few ethics topics were covered in some courses, but we were not exposed to a systematic model for ethical decision-making. Little attention was paid to learning how to work through ethical dilemmas we might encounter in counseling practice. Because a systematic approach to working with ethical dilemmas was lacking, I began reading and studying ethical and professional issues when I entered the counseling profession.

In the mid-1970s, I began teaching ethics classes to both undergraduates and graduate students. Many students approached the ethics course with fear and trepidation, wanting to stay out of trouble with licensing boards and with upset clients who might file a malpractice suit. At the beginning of my course, students did not want to struggle with ambiguity; instead, they expected definite answers. One of my goals in teaching ethics is to assist students in creating a way to think about making ethical decisions. Rather than considering each ethical question separately, I focused on teaching a model that would enable students to explore the various facets of any ethical question or dilemma. We talked about the purpose of ethics codes and the role codes of ethics play in ethical decision-making. Students eventually came to accept the fact that simply learning the ethics codes does not necessarily ensure ethical practice. They realized that ethics codes cannot be applied in a rote manner because each client's situation is unique and will likely call for a solution that demands professional judgment. Although my students initially expected an ethics course to entail memorization of facts and rules, their attitude soon changed and their enthusiasm grew for the topics and cases we explored. Having a good ethical foundation is part of being a competent counselor. If you were in my ethics class, you would hear these messages: Be willing to question and to reflect on what you are doing, remain humble, and never think you have all the right answers.

My students come to appreciate how much personal reflection is involved in thinking about ethics and that multiple answers are often available in response to an ethical question. Ethics codes provide us with information and guidance, but they do not replace critical thinking. Limiting our scope of practice to following ethical standards is not sufficient; these codes can never replace our informed professional judgment and goodwill.

Pro bono work is recommended in the ethics codes of many professional organizations. Is it unethical if I do not intend to engage in pro bono services?

The ethics codes of the National Association of Social Workers, the American Counseling Association, and the American Psychological Association all encourage practitioners to contribute to society by devoting a portion of their professional time and skills to services for which there is no expectation of significant financial return. I cannot judge your decision not to engage in pro bono services. You need to consider your life circumstances and decide for yourself how much, if any, time you are able to commit for little or no financial remuneration.

Pro bono work provides assistance to individuals who cannot afford psychological services they need, and it is also a good way to give back to the community. Working with populations who have limited financial resources can broaden your experience and stretch your set of techniques. Having the opportunity to work with client problems that may not necessarily arise with a more affluent clientele will make you a more well-rounded clinician. Pro bono work with diverse client populations also improves multicultural competence. Furthermore, engaging in pro bono work can lead to a paying job.

To broaden the discussion of the ethics involved in engaging in pro bono work, it is useful to contrast mandatory ethics with aspirational ethics. *Mandatory ethics* involves a basic level of ethical functioning in which counselors fulfill minimal standards of practice. *Aspirational ethics* describes the highest standards of practice and requires counselors to meet the spirit of the ethics code as well. Counselors who comply at the first level, mandatory ethics, are generally safe from legal action in courts of law or professional censure by state licensure boards. At the higher level of ethical functioning, aspirational ethics, counselors make a commitment to give priority to the effects their interventions have on the welfare of their clients. Counselors who practice aspirational ethics are concerned with doing as much good as possible and sharing their talents with others.

I am pleased that so many students who enroll in my ethics course are motivated to think of ways they can give back to individuals and the community. They are realistic and know they must make an adequate living, but they are also keenly interested in finding ways to strive for the highest good for people. I model ways of aspirational practice through my own pro bono efforts, such as consulting with groups that cannot not afford my fees. I often give presentations at university programs for no pay and provide Skype sessions for some of my colleagues who teach counseling at several universities each semester. It is rewarding for me to share ideas with others through these presentations without expecting a financial reward. Throughout my entire career, I have balanced my need to earn an income with my desire to offer many kinds of pro bono work. In doing this, I have no regrets.

When faced with an ethical dilemma, is there a decision-making model I can use to help me resolve the dilemma?

When you encounter an ethical dilemma, you are expected to carefully consider an ethical decision-making process. My colleagues and I reviewed a number of models various writers in the field have described, and we have conceptualized an ethical decision-making model with eight steps that you can use in working through ethical problems (see Corey, Corey, & Corey, 2019). Thinking through ethical issues is not done in a lock-step manner, and these eight procedural steps should not be thought of as a linear map to reach a resolution on ethical matters. You may circle back through some steps as you engage in discussions with clients, colleagues, faculty, or other experts. These steps are meant to stimulate self-reflection, and I urge you to remain open to new perspectives as you work through your decision process.

1. *Identify the problem or dilemma.* To determine the nature of the problem or dilemma, gather all the information that sheds light on the situation. Clarify whether the conflict is ethical, legal, clinical, cultural, professional, or moral—or a combination of any or all of these. The first step toward resolving an ethical dilemma is recognizing that a problem exists and identifying its specific nature.

2. *Identify the potential issues involved.* Evaluate the rights, responsibilities, and welfare of all those who are affected by the situation. Consider the cultural context of the situation, including relevant cultural dimensions of the client's situation such as culture, race, socioeconomic status, and religious or spiritual background. When it is appropriate, and to the degree that it is possible, involve your client in identifying potential issues in the situation.

3. *Review the relevant ethics codes.* Consider the degree to which the standards of your professional organization offer a possible solution to the problem. You can also seek guidance from your professional organization on any specific concern relating to an ethical or legal situation.

4. *Know the applicable laws and regulations.* It is necessary that you keep up to date on relevant state and federal laws that might apply to ethical dilemmas. However, realize that knowledge of the laws and regulations is not sufficient in addressing a dilemma.

5. *Obtain consultation.* You do not have to make ethical decisions alone. It is good to consult with several colleagues to obtain different perspectives on the area of concern and to arrive at the best possible decision. Consultation can give you ideas that you have not considered, and it can also help you gain objectivity. Doing this can protect you from legal liability.

6. *Consider possible and probable courses of action.* Think about the possible range of actions and identify multiple options for dealing with the situation. Consider the ethical and legal implications of the possible solutions you have identified. In thinking about the possibilities for action, discuss these options with your client as well as with other professionals, and document these discussions.

7. *Enumerate and consider the possible consequences of various decisions.* Examine the probable outcomes of various decisions, considering the potential risks and benefits of each course of action. Collaborating with your client about the consequences of various actions can lead to your client's empowerment. Realize that there are likely to be multiple outcomes rather than a single desired outcome in dealing with an ethical dilemma.

8. *Choose what appears to be the best course of action.* To decide on the best course of action, consider the information you have received. Once you have decided on a course of action, remain open to the possibility that circumstances may require that you make adjustments to your plan. Document the outcome of your decision and include any additional actions that were taken to resolve the issue. Document any consultations you had to assist you in the decision-making process.

To illustrate how this decision-making model can result in ethical practice, I will describe how Marianne and I applied this model of working through ethical concerns in one of our mutual projects.

For years, many counselor educators asked us to film a group that would bring to life the various stages in the development of a group. We wanted to make an educational video based on group members who were willing to address their own personal issues and concerns. We did not want to use actors who would follow a script nor group members who would be restricted to role-playing. We were interested in filming a 3-day intensive residential group with eight members, with the final product being a 2-hour educational video. We believed the video would be a valuable teaching tool for group counseling courses, and we gave a great deal of thought to the potential ethical problems involved in creating and implementing this program. Here are some of the measures we took to minimize exploiting or harming those who would participate in the proposed group (Step 1). The number in parenthesis refers to one of the steps in this model.

Before we launched this project, we consulted with many colleagues and counselor educators from various universities. They provided feedback on our proposal, and we considered this feedback to ensure that we did not miss any relevant ethical principles and practices in making this video. Those who reviewed our proposal were supportive of our project. By carefully considering the results of the consultations with faculty and also with those who would participate as members in the video, we were confident that we could create an actual group rather than relying on actors or a scripted program (Step 5).

One of the ethical concerns involved selecting and preparing those who would participate in this educational program. We contacted a number of former students and asked about their interest in being in this group. We told them that they were candidates for this project and that we would inform them once we decided how we could best compose a group representing various aspect of diversity.

We had a preliminary meeting with the group members we selected to explain what being part of this project would entail. In reviewing the ethics codes, a number of standards were relevant to our project: informed consent, avoiding the misuse of power, avoiding exploitation, doing no harm to the participants, and limitations of confidentiality. We wanted to make sure that those who were considering being a part of the group were fully informed about their rights and responsibilities, what they could expect from us, our expectations of them, and the safeguards put in place to ensure ethical practice. We wanted to eliminate surprises and provide clarity regarding the purpose of this educational video. The informed consent process began at the initial meeting and continued throughout the filming and editing process (Steps 2 and 3). Our primary concern was to avoid exploitation of the trust of those who would be in the group. We respected the fact that working on the members' genuine concerns would entail courage and vulnerability on their part (Step 3).

The legal aspects of this video program needed to be considered. For example, confidentiality could not be granted because the video would be viewed by many students in group counseling classes (Steps 3 and 4). All the group members were required to sign a waiver prior to filming that granted the publisher the right to distribute the program to educational institutions. As part of the informed consent process, participants had opportunities to discuss any of the legal dimensions of the project. Our concerns were more about the ethical parameters of this project than the legal aspects (Steps 4 and 7).

At a preliminary meeting prior to filming, participants were encouraged to ask questions and express concerns about what would occur during the filming and how we would select portions of the 3-day group for the 2-hour video (Steps 5 and 6). We raised questions about potential concerns group members might not have thought about, such as their visibility once the group video was shown in counseling classes. Most of the participants were entering the counseling profession, and they could be recognized at professional conferences by counseling students and their professors, and perhaps by family members and relatives (Steps 6 and 7). Participants currently in therapy were asked to consult with their therapist to explore any concerns about being a member in an intensive group that would be filmed (Step 5).

All of the participants met for a day before the filming took place for orientation and to get acquainted with us, each other, and the crew who would do the filming. Meeting with the entire group enabled us to attend to the procedures involved in filming, and once again we asked if members had any concerns before filming began the next day. We advised members that the best way to prepare for the group would be to approach it as they would a therapeutic group that was not being filmed. We let them know that they could determine what aspects of their work they did not want to be in the final program. At the end of each day throughout the filming process, members could inform us and the director that they wanted certain portions of their work deleted, and we honored their requests (Step 7). As an additional safeguard, we asked participants to contact us after the filming with any afterthoughts about including a certain part of their work in the final video. This additional safeguard gave members time and some distance from the intensity of filming to consider any reservations they had about using their work. We had a follow-up session with all the participants later on to show them the final 2-hour video. At this time, they could still request that we cut any part of their participation that they did not want to have included in the final version of the program (Steps 7 and 8).

Evolution of a Group was first released in 2000. Over the years, we have had considerable feedback from students and professors regarding how they were personally and professionally affected by viewing the video. We continue to share this feedback with the participants in the group video. Viewers have consistently indicated how they value seeing an actual group from both a personal and an academic perspective (Steps 6, 7, and 8).

Our filming project illustrates the complexity of thinking through potential ethical issues, and it shows how a systematic model like ours can be a basis for sound ethical reasoning. The goal of any ethical decision-making process is to help us take into account all relevant facts, to use any resources available to us, and to reason through ethical concerns in a way that points to the best possible course of action.

For a further discussion of the ethical decision-making process, see *Issues and Ethics in the Helping Professions* (Corey, Corey, & Corey, 2019), *Becoming a Helper* (Corey & Corey, 2021), *Ethical, Legal, and Professional Issues in Counseling* (Remley & Herlihy, 2020), and *ACA Ethical Standards Casebook* (Herlihy & Corey, 2015a). For an excellent reference on the legal aspects of ethical practice, see *The Counselor and the Law: A Guide to Legal and Ethical Practice* (Wheeler & Bertram, 2019).

Refection Questions

1. What does becoming an ethical practitioner mean to you?
2. What ways can you think of to offer pro bono work?
3. If you were to enroll in an ethics in counseling course, what expectations would you have?
4. What are your thoughts about practicing aspirational ethics?
5. What are your reactions to the ethical decision-making model we described?

Chapter 12

Boundary Issues in Counseling

Introduction

Most of us will wrestle with how to balance multiple roles in our professional relationships. A few examples of problematic concerns associated with multiple relationships include whether to barter with a client for goods or services, whether it is ever acceptable to counsel a friend or social acquaintance, how to interact with clients outside the office, and whether it is acceptable to develop a social relationship with a former client. Discussion in this chapter centers around how to establish appropriate boundaries in your work as a counselor. These topics are complex and require thinking and reasoning. Before reading the answer to each question, imagine how you would react in this situation.

• • •

What is the difference between boundary crossings and boundary violations? How can we prevent boundary crossings from resulting in boundary violations?

In my graduate program in counseling in the early 1960s, I rarely heard anything about boundaries. Few guidelines were available, and practitioners had to decide for themselves what constituted ethical practice. As ethics codes were developed, a key aspect was the importance of establishing clear boundaries for the protection of clients.

Students sometimes ask about the difference between boundary crossings and boundary violations. A *boundary crossing* is a departure from standard practice that could potentially benefit clients, whereas a *boundary violation* is a serious breach that causes harm to the client. Boundary crossings are inevitable in certain settings, and they can be beneficial. For example, a client may request that you attend a graduation because you have been instrumental in encouraging your client to complete a graduate program. Flexible boundaries can be clinically helpful when applied ethically, but boundary crossings must be evaluated on a case-by-case basis.

There are potential risks as well as benefits when crossing boundaries with clients. To minimize the *potential* for harm to clients, consider the possible ramifications to the therapeutic relationship and to your client whenever you contemplate crossing boundaries. For example, if you enter into a bartering arrangement with a client who lost her job and exploit her or take advantage of the power differential by asking for more than you give in return, this could result in a boundary violation. If you have not given considerable thought to engaging in boundary crossings, and if you have not discussed such matters with your clients and do not have clear agreements with them, you may innocently cross boundaries in ways that result in problems for both you and your clients.

When managing boundaries, I have learned how important it is to think preventively and to seek consultation with colleagues in any cases that could pose difficulties for the therapeutic relationship. My concerns are not so much of a legal nature, nor do they come from a risk management perspective. Instead, I have come to appreciate the paramount importance of carefully thinking through potentially problematic situations that could pose any risk of harming the client or taking advantage of a client's vulnerability. In addition to seeking consultation and having open discussions with colleagues about my teaching and counseling practices, I emphasize including the client or the student in a discussion of potential consequences prior to considering any form of boundary crossing and in managing boundaries effectively.

For further reading on how boundary crossings can sometimes be beneficial, I recommend *Boundaries in Psychotherapy:
Ethical and Clinical Explorations* (Zur, 2007).

What are some challenges in managing boundaries in our personal and professional lives?

Boundary issues affect the work of professional counselors in
diverse roles, including counselor educator, supervisor, agency
counselor, private practitioner, school counselor, rehabilitation
counselor, and practitioners in other specialty areas. All professionals in the helping professions must recognize and deal
with the potential difficulties inherent in dual or multiple relationships and establish and maintain appropriate boundaries
in therapeutic relationships.

Certain clients may challenge your rationale related to appropriate boundaries. Their behavior may be aimed at testing you to find out how far they can go with you. Some clients
may transgress therapeutic boundaries by trying to enter into
a friendship or develop some kind of social relationship with
you. These clients may be manifesting transference. Carefully
guard against attempts by these individuals to breach boundaries. You can do this by clearly stating your own boundaries,
knowing your role and function in the therapeutic relationship,
and avoiding relaxing appropriate boundaries to be liked by
your clients.

If you are working as a counselor, a counselor educator, a
clinical supervisor, or a counselor-in-training, you may frequently need to define and maintain clear boundaries. Interpersonal boundaries are not static and may be redefined over
time as you and your clients work closely together. Boundaries
are not meant to be walls that separate you from your clients.
Clear boundaries provide structure to your relationships and
safeguard clients. Boundary problems can result in harm to clients, students, and supervisees, and they also create distress in
those who hold more power in the professional relationship.
Creating and maintaining healthy boundaries, both personally
and professionally, is one way to practice self-care.

Boundary issues can extend beyond the professional realm
and affect your personal life too. If you have difficulty establishing and maintaining good boundaries in your personal life,
you may encounter similar problems in forming appropriate
boundaries in your professional life. Increase your awareness

and consistently practice establishing and holding appropriate boundaries. Engaging in personal counseling, discussing issues with peers and colleagues, and exploring concerns about boundaries with supervisors are all pathways that strengthen healthy boundaries.

Are dual and multiple relationships generally unethical, and should they be avoided?

Most professional organizations have moved away from the rigid position that multiple relationships are inherently problematic and must be avoided and toward a more moderate approach. Topics such as establishing appropriate boundaries, recognizing potential conflicts of interest, and ethical means for dealing with multiple relationships have been dealt with specifically and extensively in most professional codes of ethics. However, there has been increasing recognition that multiple relationships are often complex, and a few simple and absolute answers cannot neatly resolve ethical dilemmas pertaining to boundary issues that may arise. Our task is to learn to *manage* multiple roles and responsibilities effectively rather than to *avoid* them. This entails managing the power differential inherent in counseling or training relationships, balancing boundary issues, and striving to avoid using power in ways that might cause harm to clients, students, or supervisees.

The ethics codes currently warn of the potential problems inherent in entering into multiple relationships, but they do not prohibit such relationships. Most ethics codes acknowledge that some multiple relationships are unavoidable and that they can be beneficial. However, when multiple relationships harm clients, or have the significant potential to harm or exploit clients, they are unethical. If professional boundaries become blurred, there is a strong possibility that disappointment will result for both the client and the counselor. We are responsible for monitoring ourselves and examining our motivations for engaging in multiple relationships. It is good practice to avoid entering into more than one role or one relationship with a client unless there is sound clinical justification for doing so.

For a series of readings on the topic of multiple relationships and boundaries in therapy, I recommend *Multiple Relationships in Psychotherapy and Counseling: Unavoidable, Common, and Mandatory Dual Relations in Therapy* (Zur, 2017).

Privacy is a primary concern regarding social media. What are some boundary considerations that apply to social media?

Most of us have become so accustomed to relying on technology that we don't think about the subtle ways privacy can be violated or boundaries can be inappropriately crossed. It is of the utmost importance to use caution and pay attention to ways you could unintentionally breach the privacy of your clients when using various forms of technology. As part of the informed consent process, discuss any concerns about privacy regarding communication via technology and take preventive measures so that both you and your clients agree on these boundaries. Most professional ethics codes state that mental health providers are expected to inform clients of the benefits and limitations of using technology in the counseling process. If you participate in email exchanges with your clients, you need to explore safeguards in using this mode of communication. It is wise to limit email exchanges to basic information such as an appointment time. Do not use email as a tool for exploring issues better dealt with in the therapy office.

Technology poses a host of ethical issues related to the blending of boundaries in both clients' and therapists' personal and professional lives, and social media sites have changed the complex intersection between privacy and openness. Managing boundaries takes on special meaning if you are involved in social media with your clients, and it is important that you develop a well-thought-out social media policy. Your clients or former clients may want to become friends with you on Facebook or some other platform. Accepting a "friend request" from clients presents potential ethical problems. It is a good practice to create separate personal and professional pages to establish clear boundaries and to avoid inappropriate multiple relationships.

Just because a technology is available does not mean it is appropriate for every client. The potential benefits need to be greater than the potential risks for clients to ethically justify any form of technology used for counseling purposes.

For selected readings on this topic, see "Multiple Relationships in a Digital World: Unprecedented Ethical and Risk Management Challenges" (Reamer, 2017) and "Digital and Social Media Multiple Relationships on the Internet" (Kolmes, 2017).

What do you do when a client touches you?

The answer to this question depends on *where, when, how,* and *why* a client touches you. It could be a gentle touch at the end of a session to express gratitude to you or a gesture of feeling in contact with you. On the other end of the spectrum, a client's touch could be a flirtatious gesture or wanting to be reassured by you. Pay attention to your reactions to a client's touch, and avoid making assumptions about the client's motivation for touching you without checking with your client. Be honest with your client about your reactions to touch, but avoid being judgmental. If you feel uncomfortable with your client's touch, talk about this with your client, which may be necessary from a therapeutic standpoint. Touching should not be used as a therapeutic technique, and you need to establish boundaries that offer safety to both you and your client. If you are just beginning to work with clients, bring up issues regarding clients' touching in your supervision sessions.

Students have asked what to do if they are not comfortable with clients who want to embrace them. I suggest that they explore their discomfort with the client and explore the client's motivation for wanting frequent embraces. I don't recommend embracing a client if doing so is not genuine for you. Trust your own subjective sense about the appropriateness and purpose of a hug. Your client will sense your unease if you are not comfortable with physical contact. Deal with this matter sensitively so your client does not feel rejected if you don't reciprocate an embrace.

What is the therapeutic value of nonerotic touching in counseling?

In the past, many incidences of therapists touching clients were motivated by the gratification of therapists' needs, not as an expression of caring and compassion for their clients. These excesses resulted in professional organizations cautioning therapists about the dangers of physical contact between counselors and clients on the grounds that touching can promote dependency, can be misunderstood by clients, and can become sexualized. Then the pendulum swung in the other direction, and counselors became leery of engaging in any touching because they feared litigation. As a result, many counselors are hesitant to engage in any kind of touching beyond a handshake. I believe nonerotic touching can be appropriate and can have significant therapeutic value for some clients in certain situations, whereas the same kind of touch may be inappropriate and harmful for other clients.

I recommend exercising more caution about engaging in touching clients when you are doing your internships or are a new professional. With increased clinical experience, you will develop your own guidelines in assessing the therapeutic value of touching. Touch needs to be evaluated in the context of client factors, the professional setting, the counselor's theoretical orientation, and the quality of the therapeutic relationship. Client factors to consider include gender, age, culture, class, personal history with touch, presenting problem, and diagnosis.

It is critical to carefully assess the appropriateness of touching clients and your motivations for any touching. Clients from an abusive background may interpret any physical contact as having sexual overtones or as an expression of dominance. Therapists must use caution when it comes to physical contact with clients because therapists cannot know how clients will interpret or react to touch.

In deciding whether to use touch in counseling, therapists need to determine whose needs are being met. If touching occurs, it should be spontaneous, nonsexual, an honest expression of the counselor's feelings, and always done for the client's benefit. It is a good idea to ask permission prior to touching your client, especially if the person has any kind of sexual trauma history. Touching should never be an unwanted gesture that results in the client feeling uncomfortable or violated.

What do you do if you see your client outside of the office?

Context is important, and there are no simple answers. If you work in a small community, or if your residence is close to where your work, you are more likely to encounter clients during their daily activities. Talk with clients before this is likely to occur and simply ask them, "How would you like me to respond if I see you outside the office?" It is not a good idea to carry on a conversation with clients you meet in the grocery store or at a community event. Remind clients that neither you nor they should initiate conversations that best belong in a counseling session. In most situations, let your client take the lead; be friendly, but keep these exchanges brief. If you observe your client's behavior outside of the office and it is not congruent with what you know about the client from your work in sessions, I don't recommend that you bring up what you observed outside of your professional relationship.

Is it appropriate to accept gifts from clients? If so, when and under what circumstances? When might it be problematic?

Most professional ethics codes had been silent on the matter of giving or receiving gifts in the therapeutic relationship, but several professional codes of ethics now address this topic. Many cultures have rituals regarding gift exchanges that may be different from your own experience. If you reject a reasonable gift, or at times withhold giving a gift, consider whether this could be perceived as a rejection of the client's culture. The practice of accepting gifts from a client must be considered within the context of these questions.

- *When is the offering of a gift occurring?* Accepting gifts from clients during the initial phase of counseling is problematic, but at the termination of counseling it might be appropriate. Know when accepting a gift from a client is clinically contraindicated, and be willing to discuss this with your client. Explore the client's motivation for offering you a gift.
- *What are the cultural implications of offering a gift?* In working with culturally diverse client populations, you may find that you need to engage in boundary crossings to enhance the counseling relationship. The cultural context plays a key role in evaluating the appropriateness of accepting a gift from a client. In some cultures, giving gifts is the norm as a way to express appreciation. Some clients would feel insulted if you were not to accept a gift.
- *What is the monetary value of the gift?* Accepting a very expensive gift is generally problematic and unethical. An inexpensive gift can be a token of appreciation.

Some therapists have given clients a small gift toward the termination of the professional relationship. Such a gift from the therapist can symbolize a key aspect of the progress the client made over the course of therapy. Or the gift could serve as a reminder of a significant lesson learned and be an expression of appreciation for the client's courage.

What do you recommend when a client frequently tries to give a gift? I am a new counselor, and I feel uneasy about this.

If you feel uncomfortable in this situation, it is not wise to ignore your feelings. A frank discussion with your client can be a key part of the therapy process. Ask the client to talk about the meaning of giving gifts to you. Do not be pressured into going against your better judgment. Establish clear boundaries with your client regarding gift giving, and explain that this is for the client's safety and to enhance the therapeutic relationship. If this situation happens with several of your clients, however, I suggest that you look at your own behavior and the messages you are sending to your clients.

If I find myself emotionally or sexually attracted to a client, does this mean I am unprofessional?

You might well feel guilty over an attraction toward a client, and you could feel uncomfortable if you sense that a client is attracted to you. If you treat these sexual feelings as if they shouldn't exist, you will not be able to address your own attraction nor that of your client. Feelings of emotional or sexual attraction do not mean that you have made therapeutic errors or that you are unethical. It is important, however, to acknowledge your feelings to yourself but certainly not to your client. Above all, avoid developing inappropriate sexual intimacies with a client. Although transient sexual feelings are normal, intense preoccupation with clients is problematic. Sexual intimacies with clients are always unethical, illegal, and harmful to clients. This applies to both current clients and former clients.

Simply experiencing sexual attraction to a client, without acting on your attraction, may result in you feeling guilty and anxious. Although you may want to hide such feelings from your supervisor or a colleague, I encourage you to take the courageous stand of acknowledging your feelings and bringing them into supervision, or talk with a trusted colleague about how you are dealing with the attraction. You might consider bringing this matter to your own therapy, especially if you find that you frequently develop intense attractions to clients. These steps can be instrumental in enabling you to manage your attractions.

How do I most effectively work with clients who express attraction to me?

Pay attention to how clients disclose their attraction to you. It may be a simple matter of appreciating your warmth and regard for them. They may wish that some individuals in their personal life were as engaging as you are. Your clients probably only see you once a week, and they may idealize you. Some clients may be flirting with you to test your boundaries. It is important that you understand the underlying motivation and manner of expression when clients disclose their attraction toward you. If a client finds you attractive and then admits feeling uncomfortable about admitting this attraction, discuss your reactions to your client's disclosure. In this situation, do not talk with your client about your attraction or absence of attraction.

For further reading on the topics addressed in this chapter, see *Boundary Issues in Counseling: Multiple Roles and Responsibilities* (Herlihy & Corey, 2015b) and *ACA Ethical Standards Casebook* (Herlihy & Corey, 2015a).

Reflection Questions

1. When you think of establishing and maintaining boundaries with clients, what are your major concerns?
2. How effective are you in managing boundaries in your personal life? What implications are there for you when it comes to managing boundaries in your professional life?
3. What are your thoughts about the use of touch in counseling?
4. What guidelines can you think of with respect to accepting gifts from your clients?
5. Can you think of a few examples of boundary crossings that you might be willing to engage in with clients?

Chapter 13

Values in Counseling

Introduction

It is crucial for counselors to clearly understand their own values and how their values influence their work with clients, sometimes even unconsciously. We have an ethical responsibility to avoid unduly influencing clients. We can best work with clients by understanding the values clients hold and assisting them in determining the degree to which their current behavior is congruent with their value system. It is the clients' place to decide if their values are working for them and for others in their life. As you read my answers to the questions in this chapter, would your answers be different from mine?

• • •

How can we best work with clients whose values are very different from our own?

Professional counselors should be able to work effectively with people manifesting a diversity of worldviews, beliefs, and intersecting cultural identities. Value differences are not ethical grounds for a referral. It is not our role to agree or disagree with clients' values, nor is it our responsibility to make judgments about their values. Counselors are expected to work through value conflicts and to focus their work on the client's values rather than their own. When you recognize instances of value conflicts, reflect on this question: "Why is it necessary that there be congruence between my value system and that of my client?" If you become aware of a conflict of values, explore your difficulties with a supervisor or by seeking consultation. It is possible to work through such conflicts successfully. Merely disagreeing with a client or not particularly liking what a client is proposing to do should not be problematic. If you are unwilling to counsel the wide range of clients you are likely to encounter, consider what is getting in your way of being objective and make the welfare of the client your priority.

I have been asked how I manage situations in which potential value conflicts occur, but in all honesty, I cannot recall any value conflicts in my counseling practice. To be sure, I have had value differences with clients, but these differences have not proven to be problematic. This is somewhat surprising because I was raised in a Catholic family and was exposed to Catholic schooling from grade school to graduate school. Catholic schooling involved dogmatic teaching to instill absolute values. I was not encouraged to question authority but to accept it. I didn't question many of the values I held until I began my teaching career. Many of my fellow teachers had very different views on life than mine, and some of these colleagues challenged my somewhat narrow thinking. I began to question many of the dogmatic beliefs I had incorporated, and in my personal therapy, I was often challenged to critically evaluate the basis for my beliefs.

Neither my father nor my mother were judgmental people; they were very open and accepting of others for their time. Their influence helped me to acquire an accepting stance and not to judge people who were different from me. In my 30s at the beginning of my counseling career, my belief system was increasingly flexible, and I learned to accept people who embraced a wide spectrum of values and worldviews. In short, I realized that I did not have to assume a judgmental role in my professional life or in my personal life. In my work as a counselor, asking myself why clients are coming to counseling has enabled me to put any difference of values into perspective. My life experiences and evolution as a professional counselor have convinced me that my role as a counselor is not to evaluate the value systems of my clients. As counselors, we should keep in mind that *it is not about us,* but about our clients!

For a resource on the ethics of counselor imposition of values and referrals based on value conflicts, see the *ACA Code of Ethics* (American Counseling Association, 2014). For readings on this topic, see *ACA Ethical Standards Casebook* (Herlihy & Corey, 2015a).

When is it appropriate to refer a client?

Referrals should be infrequent and suggested only after a thoughtful review of the situation. It is good practice to reflect on your reasons for wanting to suggest a referral. A referral may be in order if a client decides you are not the best therapist for him or her at this time. However, before too quickly referring, it is important to explore the client's reasons for wanting to switch to another therapist. When you do not have the knowledge, skills, education, or training required to competently treat a client, a referral is the ethical course of action.

I believe it is dishonest for counselors to contend they are not competent to treat certain clients when their real reason for wanting to refer a client is due to a conflict of values. For example, referral is inappropriate and unethical when a therapist's discomfort over value differences pertains to the sexual orientation of the client. It is not appropriate for a heterosexual counselor to refer a gay client to another counselor because of the moral or religious values the counselor holds pertaining to same gender relationships.

At presentations I have given, I have been asked if it is acceptable for counselors practicing in a state where legislation grants "freedom of conscience" to refer clients if the counselors hold personal values that would make it difficult for them to work with those clients. For example, a 2016 Tennessee law allows therapists with "sincerely held principles" to deny services to potential clients who identify as lesbian, gay, bisexual, or transgender without risk of legal consequences. As long as reluctant practitioners refer the client to another qualified professional, the referring counselor will be protected from licensure suspensions and any legal penalties. These counselors may be protected from legal actions for refusing services to clients who violate their "sincerely held principles," but I contend that they are not protected from an ethical violation. The ethics codes of most professional organizations make it clear that discrimination—behaving differently and unfairly toward a specific group of people—is unethical and unacceptable. It is our responsibility to become aware of our personal prejudices and biases regarding sexual orientation and bracket our values and manage value differences we may have rather than refusing to work with certain individuals. This is particularly important when a client discloses his or her sexual orientation after the therapy relationship is firmly established. This judgmental attitude on the part of the counselor can seriously harm a client in that situation. Keeping your values separate from your work with clients in no way implies that you need to surrender or change your own values.

For a more complete discussion of ethical bracketing, see *Ethical, Legal, and Professional Issues in Counseling* (Remley & Herlihy, 2020) and *Becoming a Helper* (Corey & Corey, 2021).

What is the role of religious and spiritual values in counseling?

Spiritual and religious values may play a major role in an individual's search for meaning in life. Clients' spiritual values should be viewed as a potential resource in therapy rather than being ignored. Part of being culturally competent involves being able to work effectively and ethically with clients' spiritual and religious concerns. Although it is important to be open in dealing with spiritual and religious themes in counseling, ethical practice requires counselors to be cautious about introducing these themes to clients and to be aware of the potential for countertransference. Some counselors may push their spiritual or religious beliefs, and other counselors may impose their nonreligious or antireligious attitudes. Neither of these approaches is ethical.

We also have an ethical responsibility to deal effectively with nonreligious clients. Some clients may have no ties to religion, others may claim that neither spirituality nor religion is important to them, still others may be atheists, and some may express anger and pain regarding their religious background. In the assessment process, it is important to ask clients how they find meaning in their lives and what resources have helped them when they have faced difficult situations. The most ethical path is to let our clients lead the way and tell us their concerns and what they want to explore in therapy. If clients say they want to talk about religious or nonreligious matters, these concerns should be addressed in their therapy.

For excellent discussions of ethically incorporating spirituality and religion in counseling, see *Integrating Spirituality and Religion Into Counseling* (Cashwell & Young, 2020) and *Spirituality in Counseling and Psychotherapy: An Integrative Approach That Empowers Clients* (Johnson, 2013).

As a group counselor, how do my values influence my interventions?

I can increase my effectiveness as a group counselor by becoming aware of my values and the subtle and direct ways I might influence group members. Although it may be difficult at times, I need to maintain my objectivity. I consistently find that participants in my groups bring a wide variety of value-laden issues for exploration, such as religion, spirituality, sexual orientation, abortion, divorce, and family problems. The purpose of the group is to assist members in clarifying their beliefs and examining options that are most congruent with their own value system. I view it as unethical for me to impose my value perspective on members. I need to remind myself that it is the group members, not I, who must live with the consequences of the choices and changes they make. I also have an ethical responsibility to prevent members from unduly influencing other members or imposing their agenda on other members.

I may hold a very different set of values from certain members in my group, but it is my ethical obligation to assist them in meeting goals that are consistent with *their* worldview and values, not my own. For example, I place a value on striving for autonomy and making choices that influence my destiny. It took me some time to understand that group members may hold collectivistic values that place a premium on making decisions that will enhance the good of their extended family. I eventually realized that independence and self-determination were my values but that those values may not be shared by all group members. In working with diversity in my groups, I concluded that I am better able to help members discover what is right for them if I can understand and appreciate their values and work within their worldview. When I have been inclined to promote my values, it has helped for me to ask myself why my clients need to adopt my perspective on life. I have concluded that if and when a value difference occurs that could potentially present a challenge for me, the best course to follow is to seek consultation in working through the situation so I can provide the appropriate standard of care.

A more complete discussion of therapists managing their values is found in *Issues and Ethics in the Helping Professions* (Corey, Corey, & Corey, 2019); for more on how a group leader's values influence the practice of group counseling, see *Groups: Process and Practice* (Corey, Corey, & Corey, 2018).

Reflection Questions

1. Can you think of a value you hold that you might want to impose on your clients, even in subtle ways?
2. What challenges, if any, do you expect to encounter in managing value conflicts with clients?
3. What are some things you can do to expand your awareness of your values and how they might influence your work as a counselor? What role do you want your values to play in your work as a counselor?
4. In what circumstances would you consider referring a client to another professional?
5. How comfortable would you be in addressing a client's problems associated with religious or spiritual values?

Chapter 14

Multicultural Issues in Counseling

Introduction

During graduate school and in your early career, it is important to be open to meeting individuals who differ from you in various ways. You do not need to share the same background, life circumstances, or worldview as your client, but you will need to have a range of experiences to draw on in understanding and appreciating all forms of diversity. If you understand how your own cultural background has contributed to who you are, you have a basis for understanding people with different worldviews. Adopting a perspective that cultural differences are positive attributes that enhance relationships will expand your ability to work with diverse client groups. As you read this chapter, reflect on life experiences you have had that will enable you to understand and appreciate the many different forms of diversity.

• • •

Why is recognizing cultural tunnel vision essential?

Many of us grow up with cultural tunnel vision. If our cultural experiences are limited, we may harbor inappropriate generalizations about unfamiliar groups. If we hope to widen our cultural perspective and reach clients with different life experiences, we must first recognize some of the ways our cultural vision is restricted. It is not helpful to burden ourselves with guilt over our cultural limitations. Self-blame rarely leads to self-understanding. It is more effective to take some steps toward identifying our cultural biases and understanding how they influence our perception of clients. Once we recognize our biases, we can begin to critically evaluate them. Cultural tunnel vision can be expanded to embrace people in diverse cultures if we are motivated and interested in learning more about them.

How did you move toward appreciating differences among groups?

As a child, I had only a dim awareness of my cultural identity and cultural background. Being around my extended immigrant Italian family taught me that people see the world through different eyes and express themselves in different ways. I learned about prejudice and discrimination through some of my father's experiences as an Italian immigrant. My father changed his name from Cordileone (meaning "heart of the lion") to Corey when he became a dentist because he thought people would not choose an Italian dentist. My extended Italian family encountered some discrimination, but I also observed that some family members harbored their own prejudices. Some of my relatives made disparaging remarks about certain other groups of people, and I learned that racism can be both subtle and blatant. I often felt I was on the outside in my extended family, which helped me develop compassion for people who were the target of any form of discrimination. I grew into a more caring person as I reflected on how people were often mistreated.

What suggestions do you have for counselors who want to improve their cultural competency?

Achieving cultural competency is a lifelong learning process that includes formal training, supervision, and self-reflection. Cultural competency involves considerable self-awareness and knowledge; it also entails acquiring skills for effective interventions when working in cross-cultural counseling situations. If you are unaware of how your culture influences you, it will be difficult for you to understand your client's culture and values.

Approach clients with interest, respect, and a healthy curiosity about learning more about their lives. Be open to letting your clients inform you about who they are and what the differences between you mean to them. I aim not to make assumptions about those with whom I work. Differences between my clients and me are topics for conversation. Although I have clinical expertise and specialized skills, I respect the idea that my clients are the experts on their own life.

Students sometimes unrealistically think they have to share the same life experiences and cultural background as their clients if they hope to connect with them. If you expect that you cannot establish working alliances with clients who are different from you, you will have few clients. There will be many differences between you and your clients, including age, spiritual values, worldviews, socioeconomic status, educational background, ability, gender, sexual orientation, race, and ethnicity. These differences are not crucial factors in competent multicultural counseling; it is how we approach these differences with clients that counts. You do not need to have experienced the same problems as a client to engage therapeutically with him or her, but you do need to be able to tune into some of the feelings your client is expressing. To understand differences salient to your clients, invite them to tell you how certain differences influence their willingness to be open with you. An honest discussion about the impact of differences is a good way to develop a therapeutic relationship. Of paramount importance is understanding the subjective experience of clients and welcoming their explorations with you about their world.

You may inadvertently say or do something that is culturally insensitive or make an assumption that offends a client. Be open to hearing what your client has to say. A client may not challenge you but instead become silent or distant. Respectfully explore what your client's silence is about without assuming it is a sign of resistance. We all make cultural mistakes, and it is how we recover from these mistakes that is crucial in repairing the relationship. Clients are generally forgiving if we are willing to admit our mistake.

A useful resource for improving your cultural competency is *Multicultural Issues in Counseling: New Approaches to Diversity* (Lee, 2019). For a practical discussion on thriving in a graduate counseling program from a multicultural perspective, see *Surviving and Thriving in Your Counseling Program* (Austin & Austin, 2020).

How do group counselors adapt group techniques to the cultural context of members?

When I began doing group work, I had a monocultural perspective and did not consciously think about how the techniques I employed might fit or not fit with the cultural diversity of group members. I assumed that any interventions and skills I learned could be applied to any group, regardless of the differences among the members. Through regular attendance at professional conferences, continuing educational opportunities, and my relationships with culturally diverse colleagues, I soon recognized the necessity of understanding and appreciating multiculturalism in doing successful group work. The current emphasis on multiculturalism has made group workers aware of the importance of attending to the cultural context when practicing ethical and effective group work.

As a group facilitator, it is my responsibility to inform potential members of the values and norms that guide group interaction. When I am screening and selecting potential members, we discuss their concerns about responding in the here and now, expressing feelings, asking for what they want, being direct and honest, engaging in self-disclosure, being open in providing feedback to other members, improving interpersonal communication, speaking up in the group, being willing to deal with conflict, and making choices for themselves. Some of the values generally associated with group participation may not be congruent with the cultural norms of some individuals. For instance, some individuals might have difficulty being direct because their culture does not put a premium on directness. Others may experience trouble asking for group time because they want to put others first. Some members will not be comfortable making decisions for themselves without considering how their decisions may affect their extended family. Some group techniques are designed to assist members in more freely expressing their feelings, and certain members will find this difficult to do because they have learned that it is not appropriate to share feelings outside of their family. I modify my techniques to increase their congruence with the cultural norms and values of the members. Our genuine respect for the differences among members and our willingness to listen to and learn from them serve as a foundation for creating therapeutic alliances within the group.

Group therapists have a responsibility to educate the members about their right to participate or not in certain techniques or exercises. Group members may choose not to participate in some exercises but may feel pressured to do what others are doing. Suggest options regarding how reluctant members may participate in a more limited way. It is a good idea to mention options whenever it is appropriate.

For further reading on adapting group techniques to the cultural context of the members, see *Group Techniques* (Corey, Corey, Callanan, & Russell, 2015).

Have you ever witnessed members committing or receiving microaggressions in your group work? If so, how did you handle it?

A microaggression is a comment or an action that individuals perceive as insulting, offensive, or inappropriate based on their personal history. Those who commit microaggressions are often not aware of how offensive and hurtful these action are for the recipients. When microaggressions occur in a group, I facilitate interactions that have the potential for providing a teaching moment. For example, a Caucasian woman in my group said to a member who was a person of color, "I don't see color. I just see you as a person. I am color blind." No one in the group reacted to this comment, so my coleader invited members to tell Toni their reactions to what she said. Joel said to Toni, "I have a problem with you saying you are color blind and that everybody is the same. I want you to see my color. I feel that you are trying to deny that stereotypes and discrimination exist. I want you to know that people of color do struggle in this society." Another person of color, Galo, had a strong reaction to what Toni said and let her know that he disagrees that all people are treated equally. He wanted her to understand that he is different in several ways: he is a different color, he has a different culture, he expresses himself in a different way, and he has a different set of beliefs. These examples illustrate that members frequently do not directly address the person who made the offensive remark even though they may feel hurt or angry. Effective group leaders encourage discussion rather than letting the moment slide by without comment.

When microaggressions based on gender take place in groups, this is an opportunity for all members to learn something more about gender awareness and gender sensitivity. A man who was the director of an agency with many women on the staff consistently referred to the women he supervised as "girls." Finally, one of the female group members let him know she found his reference to women as girls offensive. He did not understand "what the big deal was about." He could see nothing wrong with calling women in his organization girls. This response to a microaggression began a group dialogue about gender role bias on the part of both women and men. For more on microaggressions, see *Counseling the Culturally Diverse* (Sue, Sue, Neville, & Smith, 2019).

Are cultural differences a barrier or a bridge to building good relationships?

Differences between people do not have to be a barrier to mutual understanding; they can actually enhance therapeutic relationships. My students often raised concerns about working with people who were different from them. They expressed doubts about their ability to create a trusting and safe environment with individuals from very different cultural backgrounds. They wondered whether they knew enough about the culture of these clients, and they were concerned about making culturally appropriate interventions. I tell my students to invite clients to tell them about the meaning of any differences between them, and especially to talk about what differences could become barriers that block understanding. If we let clients lead the way, we will learn how best to work with differences in a way that facilitates the counseling process.

I have a personal perspective on how differences in an intimate relationship can be successfully managed. About 60 years ago I was convinced that differences between Marianne and me presented a challenge in considering marriage. She is German, and I am Italian. She is from a small village in Germany, and I am from Los Angeles. She is Protestant, and I am Catholic. Although we shared many values, our personalities were quite different. What helped us work effectively with our differences was to recognize them, to understand the ways we were different, to appreciate our differences, and most important of all, to be willing to talk about how our differences would play out in our marriage. It was important to come to some basic agreement regarding religion, and we agreed not to attempt to convert each other. We continued to talk about critical issues and were able to come to terms with how we would deal with certain differences. From my personal experience, I can attest to the fact that differences can enhance a personal relationship if those differences are respected, acknowledged, and addressed.

What are key advocacy responsibilities and roles for counselors?

Counselors often focus on the inner conflicts of their clients and fail to recognize the importance of environmental realities that contribute to the problems clients bring to therapy. Some client problems result from being disenfranchised, as individuals or as members of a group, from systems that withhold valued resources from them. There are injustices in society, and discrimination and oppression are realities that should be a topic for discussion in the therapeutic endeavor. Counselors need to be willing to address social injustices and the effects they have on clients.

Becoming an advocate for clients is a role you might consider adopting even though this may seem overwhelming. Help clients learn to find their voice and to use their voice to bring about change. For example, first-generation students may not take steps toward applying for graduate studies in counseling or social work because they do not understand how graduate programs operate. Faculty can help these students identify barriers that might prevent them from gaining entry into a graduate program. Through mentoring and advocacy efforts by concerned faculty members, students can learn specific skills for challenging these barriers. Encourage clients to advocate for themselves by discussing actions they can take in dealing with environmental barriers that prevent them from reaching their personal goals.

For more on social justice and advocacy, see *Counseling for Social Justice* (Lee, 2018).

What are some "aha" moments you have experienced when working in a foreign country?

Teaching in a foreign country provides many opportunities to see things from a new perspective. Marianne and I conducted a workshop with a large group of mental health workers in Hong Kong, and I asked the participants to raise questions after a live demonstration of a group session. We invited questions and observations about the group process and our interventions. No one responded. We repeated our request, and still no questions or comments were forthcoming. We then tried another approach. We asked the audience to form small groups and to talk with each other about what they had observed. In this setting, they were extremely engaged and very willing to talk about their reactions and observations; they even formulated questions. A spokesperson from each small group gave a summary for their group when we reconvened. We were impressed with their insights, observations, and questions. Eventually, the participants let us know that they did not feel comfortable individually asking questions or evaluating our demonstration, but they were eager to discuss the presentation and list specific points as a group. This reminded us that working in small groups is often more effective than focusing on individuals in a collectivistic culture.

Marianne and I learned a cultural lesson about avoiding assuming we know the meaning of a behavior when we were teaching in Korea. We were conducting a 3-day therapy group with eight members. The sessions were being videotaped and streamed into an adjoining room for a large number of observers. On the second day, we began the group by asking members to say something about their experience the first day and to mention any afterthoughts they had about what had occurred within the group. The members were silent. We tried many different ways to get a sense of how the group members were affected and how they were approaching returning to the group, only to encounter silence. I was busy having an inner dialogue and wondering what the silence meant. Did they have regrets about their participation on the first day? Were they uncomfortable with the emotions they experienced and expressed in the group? Were they intimidated by the professionals who were observing them in the other room? Did they have concerns about what we as group facilitators might be thinking about them? As we continued to explore what the silence might mean, we finally learned that they were self-conscious about how well they spoke English with other Koreans observing the session. They feared that the observers might be judging them because of their grammar. In fact, several of the members said they had rehearsed translating what they wanted to say from Korean into English so they would not be judged unintelligent for the way they spoke English. It did not occur to me that their reluctance to speak centered on their concern about speaking English. This reminded me again to avoid interpreting or assigning meaning to an event before respectfully and patiently exploring the underlying reasons for clients' behavior.

Both Marianne and I have taught group counseling and done intensive in-service experiential groups in Ireland for counselors who wanted to gain additional experience and competence in group work. Our training groups were structured to meet all day, and we generally included short breaks during the day. We soon learned that Irish "tea breaks" were precious to them, and they typically wanted more time than we had allotted. I would do my best to gather them up after about 15 to 20 minutes because we had a full teaching agenda. I quickly learned that the participants had their own agenda, and that pushing my agenda had counterproductive results. During tea breaks, participants reached out to some of the people they did not know, and it was important for them to socialize. This was a good lesson for me to be mindful of a culture different from my own and not to push the river but to let it flow at its own rate.

A last cultural insight that I want to share involves a time when Marianne and I were conducting a 1-week intensive group for counselors who practiced in Mexico. On the first day, many members arrived late, some said they would need to miss a half day, and a few indicated they would have to miss the final day. I stressed the importance of attending all sessions and arriving on time because I believed the entire group needs to work together for cohesion to form. Despite my concern, which I expressed at the initial meeting, group members did exactly as they said they would do. It was a great challenge for me to simply let the process unfold. I was extremely surprised to discover that this group showed a high degree of trust and cohesiveness. Not only did they learn a lot, so did we as coleaders. On the last day of the workshop, the participants humored me by all showing up and all being on time!

These cultural learning experiences taught me that sometimes my agenda for a group is not the agenda of the group members. In each of these experiences, I learned how important it is to consider the cultural context for teaching and learning. My focus was on teaching workshop participants about counseling, but had I adapted my teaching style and approach to fit the culture of the participants, more learning could have taken place. Expecting members to adapt to my style of teaching was ethnocentric and perhaps a bit egocentric as well.

Reflection Questions

1. How aware are you of your cultural identity and cultural background? What importance do you place on this awareness in understanding clients who are culturally different from you?
2. To what degree do you think you have cultural tunnel vision? What can you do to broaden your vision?
3. When you read that acquiring and improving cultural competency is a lifelong learning process, what are your thoughts?
4. What life experiences can you draw from to understand the diverse range of client problems you will encounter?
5. What are you learning in your program about becoming a multiculturally competent counselor?

Chapter 15

Self-Doubt and Learning From Mistakes

Introduction

Becoming the best therapist you can be does not mean being perfect. I counsel students to accept themselves as growing and maturing professionals and to learn what they can from any mistakes along the way. Being perfect is an unrealistic standard. I suggest to mentees and students that a realistic goal is to know that you can control your quest for perfection rather than letting it control you. We do not need to be perfect to accomplish a great deal in our personal and professional lives. The overarching themes in this chapter are learning to control the need to be perfect, challenging self-doubt, and viewing mistakes as an opportunity for learning.

• • •

How can a new intern or professional deal with self-doubt when it feels like we have no idea what we're doing?

When you begin your internship, you are not expected to know everything. Give yourself credit for the basic counseling skills you have learned. You will acquire and refine new skills during your internship. If you tell yourself that you have no idea what you are doing, you are probably being overly self-critical. You already have some sense of how to intervene, and you can begin to follow your intuition and see what happens. It is *not* a good idea to share the following comment with your client: "I have no idea what I am doing!" Writing and reflecting on your self-talk and your self-doubts can be useful. I highly recommend keeping a journal and suggest that you write about situations with clients that trigger your anxiety and other emotions. Expecting to do all the work and being a stellar therapist is bound to get in the way of establishing a positive working alliance.

Most of us experience self-doubt, especially when we first begin counseling others. When I first began seeing clients, I wondered if I had made a poor choice by thinking I could become an effective counselor. Don't let self-doubt immobilize you. Catch yourself when you begin to wonder if you are cut out to be a counselor, and reflect on the basis for doubting yourself. Some degree of performance anxiety is to be expected, and what you do about this anxiety is important. If you talk about your performance anxiety with your supervisor or your peers, you are likely to discover that performance anxiety is not unique to you. As a beginning counselor, I doubted my counseling skills and had a high level of anxiety around making the right interventions and saying the right things to clients. I am pleased that I did not give in to my doubts and switch careers too soon.

How can I correct my mistakes and maintain self-love in the process?

Even seasoned counselors make interventions with clients that are not productive. Not all mistakes need to be corrected. I prefer to look at these unsuccessful interventions as ideas that were not creative, useful, or helpful rather than labeling them mistakes. If you are not open to the possibility of making mistakes, you will seriously limit the scope of your interventions with clients. The problem is not in making mistakes but in failing to learn from those mistakes. Refusing to acknowledge a mistake that may have occurred is likely to get in the way of becoming an effective counselor. Most mistakes are only missed opportunities, such as showing a lack of sensitivity, failing to be fully present, or introducing a good technique in an untimely way. Mistakes can be opportunities for growth that push you to make constructive changes in what you are doing. Being open to learning involves the risk that an intervention may not work out as anticipated. We need to recognize and acknowledge mistakes, attempt to understand what went wrong, and consider alternative ways to approach the client.

Some years ago I was considering an offer to do a series of workshops in South Korea. I knew translators would be assisting me, and I was fretting over how to present my material and keep the flow of my ideas going through the translating process. Even though I studied books about the customs and traditions of the Korean people, I was concerned about making cultural errors. I talked with a couple of colleagues who had traveled to other countries and worked with translators in their workshops. They assured me that indeed I would make some cultural errors but that I should not exaggerate my worry about this. They convinced me that my crucial task lay in how I recovered from any mistakes I made. From this experience, I learned the value of relinquishing control and letting the translators I worked with guide me in this new experience. I found that most people were forgiving of any cultural faux pas I committed, which freed me to be more myself and not become immobilized by the fear of saying and doing the wrong thing.

Accept the fact that you will inevitably make interventions that do not go as well as expected or that you will make insensitive remarks to a client or that you will make an inaccurate interpretation. Admit your oversights or errors to clients, and do not let a mistake derail you. Your self-worth is not contingent on doing everything exceptionally well. Offending a client does not have to ruin the relationship. You can repair a rupture in the therapeutic alliance by talking with your client about how your actions or words were viewed as offensive and how you could be more mindful in the future.

How do I best deal with my desire to try to fix my client?

I am not fond of the concept of "fixing clients." I have learned that most clients need someone to listen to them and to understand them on a deep level. If I am able to listen with interest and demonstrate that I understand what my clients are sharing, I am doing my job. Considerable healing takes place when we strive to understand people and have confidence that they are capable of finding their own way.

Some people who seek counseling want advice or concrete answers to their problems, and these clients need to be educated about your view of the counseling process. Your counseling approach may have a problem-solving orientation, but that doesn't mean people who seek your assistance need fixing in any way. If your tendency is to give clients answers or advice or to direct how they live their life, it is time to examine what is behind your need to quickly resolve the problems your clients present. You may be uncomfortable watching people struggle or suffer, and this may lead you to intervene in a way that reassures or makes clients feel comfortable. Sometimes silence is what a client needs, especially after experiencing intense emotions. Experiment with listening and sharing your reactions to what you hear your client express, but resist the inclination to wrap up the problem quickly and neatly. Clients have inner resources, and you can help them find their own solutions. Listening to your clients and letting them lead the way is therapeutic in itself and can result in life-changing experiences.

What do I do if my mind goes blank in an individual session with a client?

We all have experienced moments when we scan our mind and find nothing there. I hope you do not let this trouble you, and I can assure you that I experience this sometimes when I am teaching a class or giving a presentation at a conference. You may momentarily lose track of what your client is saying or forget the point you were trying to make. Most clients will forgive you for losing concentration if you willingly acknowledge these momentary lapses rather than trying to hide them. It is another matter entirely if you find your mind wandering excessively with a particular client, or if this is a frequent occurrence with many clients. This may indicate that you are trying to do too much at once or that you are preoccupied with too many demands at work. Clients deserve our presence. Spend a moment becoming centered before each counseling session so you will be able to bring yourself into the present moment.

What do you do if you temporarily zone out and miss something important and the client knows it?

Being fully present with clients in counseling sessions is a worthy goal. We can practice mindfulness skills and center ourselves before we meet with a client, even if we have only a few minutes before a session, and this can help us sustain our focus throughout the session. However, no matter how skilled we are, we will occasionally drift away from present awareness. If a client notices this and brings it to our attention, we can shift our focus back to the client and repair this lapse. It is a good practice to allow some time toward the end of the session to ask clients to share what their experience was like during the session. Routinely asking for client feedback enables us to make any necessary modifications to enhance our interventions going forward. Listen to client feedback nondefensively and consider what clients are telling us. Most clients will appreciate our honesty and our attempts to be as present as possible, and they are likely to forgive momentary inattention on our part if they feel we are engaged with them.

How can striving for perfectionism get in the way of success?

As a neophyte counseling professional, I could not imagine myself being as skilled and insightful as I perceived my mentors and teachers to be. I measured myself against their polished abilities and came up short. I viewed them as being close to perfect and perceived myself as imperfect. It was difficult for me to be fully present with clients when I was overly concerned with how I was coming across and what my teachers might be thinking about me. I wanted approval and to be liked, and I tried to figure out what others expected of me so I could give them what they wanted. I was much more aware of myself than I was of the client sitting before me. With supervision and personal therapy, over time I tamed my inner critic, and I learned the difference between aiming for perfection and striving for excellence. I came to believe that doing my best, working diligently in acquiring skills, and being disciplined in deliberate practice was my best way forward. Demanding perfect performances at all times is a sure route to exhaustion, burnout, and stifled creativity.

Perfectionistic behavior often starts before we enter graduate school, and it can persist throughout our educational and professional careers. Perfectionistic strivings drive behavior but often sabotage success. Graduate students tend to be perfectionists and place an inordinate measure of their worth on getting an A grade. Some students equate anything less than an A with failure. In my doctoral program, learning did not always come easy, and I was certainly not a straight A student. My graduate record reveals that I earned 14 A and 11 B grades in my courses. I am pleased that I did not let my share of B grades deter my interest in pursuing a doctorate in counseling. I was more concerned with what I was learning in my courses than merely with the grade I received. As a professor, I do my best to assure students that stressing over achieving an A is not a measure of their ability or their potential as future counselors. I urge my students not to make grades their index of success.

A good resource for learning to accept imperfection and living with failure is *On Being a Therapist* (Kottler, 2017).

How can I deal with my insecurities about being competent?

Becoming a competent professional is a lifelong process, not a one-time event. Feelings of insecurity are very common at the beginning of your career. Sometimes you will be excited about your future as a counseling professional, and at other times you may be discouraged and wonder if it is all worth the effort. Accept that some insecurity is to be expected, and don't let it burden you. In fact, I worry more about students who seem overly confident and have an unrealistic view of their capabilities. Feeling insecure in your abilities can give you the impetus to work diligently and to put your best efforts into your projects. Counselors-in-training often wonder, "Can I really do this, and how do I know I will be any good at it?" When you experience insecurities over your competence, consider what might be holding you back. Don Quixote dared "to dream the impossible dream," and pursuing your own dream can make all the difference. Do not lose sight of your vision, even when you meet with detours along the road. Believe in yourself and find sources of support and encouragement to help you through tough times. If you work diligently, your dreams will come true.

At what point in your counseling career did you finally feel confident and capable?

In my early years as a professional, I worried that my insecurities would get the best of me. Feedback from former clients who years after termination let me know that our work together had a positive impact on them has helped me feel secure in my competence. Certainly, I do not feel totally competent in all areas, but I am confident of my expertise in selected areas that I have been trained in and in which I have gained practice. Being kinder to myself and not demanding that I be completely competent at all times has enabled me to gain a more realistic picture of what competence means.

Are all failures fatal? How can we best respond to experiencing failure?

My own fear of failing, feelings of inadequacy, and struggles to define who I am have been key components of my learning how to live well. I have had my share of failures, but I have come to realize that failing in some endeavor does not mean that I am a total failure as a person. Another key lesson I learned was that making a mistake is not the same as being a failure. There are no guarantees in pursuing a professional endeavor. Alfred Adler believed that feelings of inferiority are the wellsprings of creativity. I agree with Adlerian psychologists that our striving for superiority, or a sense of personal competence, is based on our feelings of inferiority. In my own life, putting my energy and time into being professionally productive is connected at least in part to compensating for feeling inadequate in many ways during my childhood, adolescence, and young adulthood. I have used my feelings of inferiority as a motivating force for overcoming barriers in life. I stopped trying to avoid failure and feelings of inferiority and accepted these feelings as part of who I am. You might find creativity within you if you embrace all aspects of your being, including your feelings of inferiority. These feelings can be a positive and motivating force.

For further reading on the topic of recovering from mistakes and learning from failures, see *The Secrets of Exceptional Counselors* (Kottler, 2018), *Letters to a Young Therapist* (Pipher, 2003), and *Surviving and Thriving in Your Counseling Program* (Austin & Austin, 2020).

Reflection Questions

1. If you had to identify two or three self-doubts, what would they be? How does your self-doubting affect your behavior?
2. Do you see yourself as struggling with perfectionism? If so, how does this affect your performance?
3. What gets in your way of being present? What can you do to increase your capacity to be present with your clients?

4. How do you view making mistakes in your counseling practice? What concerns do you have about failing or making mistakes?

5. What does it mean to you when you read that becoming a competent counseling professional is a lifelong process rather than a one-time event?

Chapter 16

Self-Disclosure

Introduction

Appropriately and timely disclosure of aspects of yourself can be a powerful intervention in facilitating a process of client self-exploration. There is a distinction between self-disclosing statements (disclosing personal information about oneself) and self-involving statements (revealing personal thoughts, feelings, and reactions to the client in the context of here-and-now aspects of the counseling relationship). Letting our clients know how we are affected by what they are saying and doing is frequently more useful than revealing detailed aspects of our personal life. For example, if you are having a difficult time listening to a client, it could be useful to let the person know this: "I've noticed at times that it's difficult for me to stay connected to what you're telling me. I'm able to follow you when you talk about yourself, but I find myself losing interest when you go into great detail about all the things your husband is doing or not doing."

It can be therapeutic to talk about yourself if doing so is for a client's benefit, but it is not necessary to reveal detailed stories of your past to form a trusting relationship with others.

Inappropriate self-disclosure, such as revealing your personal problems to clients, can easily distract clients from productive self-exploration. If your self-disclosing behavior prevents clients from exploring their issues, consider dealing with this in your own therapy or supervision. As you read and reflect on the answers addressing various aspects of self-disclosure, formulate your own guidelines regarding what constitutes appropriate counselor self-disclosure.

• • •

What are some good reasons, and not so good reasons, for being self-disclosing?

The best reason for counselor self-disclosure is when doing so would benefit your client. You can assess whether self-disclosure is useful by paying attention to your client's reactions to what you reveal about yourself. Some clients may have a need to share their reservations about working with you because of a difference in age, race, gender, sexual orientation, or life experiences. Clients may ask how you are hearing and reacting to their concerns about working with you because of these differences. Self-disclosure around these differences can facilitate the therapeutic process.

A not so good reason for self-disclosing is when this satisfies your own needs rather than your client's needs. If your self-disclosure is motivated by your need to talk about yourself, this can be problematic. You also need to pay attention to maintaining boundaries. Clients may ask personal questions such as your marital status, your political leanings, whether or not you have children, your family history, what you do on your vacations, or other matters that are not relevant to the therapeutic relationship. It is generally helpful to decide what you are and are not willing to disclose prior to seeing a client, especially if you are a new counselor. I also recommend that you give some thought to how you will handle personal questions prior to seeing clients. Pausing before answering personal questions is an effective therapeutic intervention that gives you an opportunity to explore the client's motivation for posing the question. A client may be trying to figure out if you can understand and relate to him or her by asking you personal questions. This may be an unconscious motivation. It is not a good idea for you to answer personal questions if you feel pressured to do so. Be open to exploring how answering these personal questions would help your clients, and discuss their reasons for being interested in knowing something personal about you.

What are some guidelines I can use to determine the appropriateness of self-disclosure?

Many of my students struggle with determining the proper balance between disclosing too much and disclosing too little. Determining the appropriate kind and amount of self-disclosure can be problematic for seasoned counselors, and it is especially difficult for new counselors. I tell my students that determining this balance has lot to do with what is being disclosed and the timing of disclosing. When working with clients who are experiencing intense emotions, I have used a few words to tell my clients how they are affecting me. I avoid going into detail about how clients' emotions bring up similar emotions in me. I strive to keep the focus on what is beneficial to the client and how a disclosure can be useful for the person at that time.

In determining the appropriateness of self-disclosure, consider *what* to reveal, *when* to disclose, and *how much* to share. Either disclosing too little or disclosing too much can be counterproductive in establishing an effective therapeutic relationship. If you try too hard to be genuine by sharing your personal experience, you may burden your client with detailed stories that distract from the client's therapy. Although it is often useful to share something about yourself, be aware of your motivations for these disclosures. It is important to pay attention to your client's reactions as you disclose to get a sense of how the person is being affected. Letting your client know something about you personally can strengthen your client's connection with you and contribute to an authentic relationship.

The most productive form of self-disclosure is related to what is going on between you and your client in a therapy session. The skill of immediacy involves disclosing what is transpiring between you and your client in the here and now. For example, whenever your client begins to talk about her relationship with her mother, you notice that she tears up and then quickly moves to another topic. When she does this, you may lose a sense of contact with her and struggle to stay present with her in the session. Challenging your client to reflect on what she is experiencing when she is talking about her relationship with her mother can be a useful intervention. Letting her know that you have a difficult time staying present can be a facilitative intervention in the present moment. Sharing personal reactions can facilitate therapeutic progress and improve the quality of your relationship with your client. However, even when you are talking about reactions based on the therapeutic relationship, caution is necessary, and discretion and sensitivity are required in deciding what thoughts, feelings, and reactions you might reveal to your client. Any self-disclosure should be selective and tailored to the needs of the client.

How can I become part of the group and at the same time stay in the leader role?

Most of my involvement with group work is with counseling groups and training group leaders. In these groups, I view my role as assisting members in achieving their personal goals and facilitating what is taking place in the group. Sometimes members would like for me to become more involved in the group by engaging in personal self-disclosure. Generally, I do not explore my personal problems in the group. My role is that of a leader rather than a group member, and I do not share a great deal of my personal life because I have a different job in the group. It takes all of my effort to pay attention to what each member needs and what is going on in the group. I am willing to disclose my ongoing reactions and observations about group members as well as how I am affected by them. At times, I may identify with certain group members who evoke personal reactions in me, and I generally acknowledge the effect they are having on me. If it seems appropriate and useful for the group, I may share certain personal experiences and how they relate to what members are exploring in the group. Although my role differs from that of the group members, I do not hide behind a professional facade. I believe that engaging in honest, appropriate, and timely self-disclosure can fulfill the leadership function of modeling. Self-disclosure can be useful when it is intentional and keeps the attention on the group members rather than on the leader. My disclosures should always be for the benefit of the members and not to gratify my own needs.

As a group counselor, how do I determine the right balance of self-disclosure?

I don't think there is a simple answer to what constitutes appropriate self-disclosure. Much depends on the type of group you are conducting and on your style of group leadership.

Some of you may be leading groups for people coping with addictions or substance abuse. These group members are likely to want to know something about you personally as well as your academic background. If you are in recovery yourself, you may decide to make this known to your group. Your personal journey could be a resource for members who are learning to manage their addiction. Your openness about what you have personally learned about addictions can go a long way toward establishing trust. Of course, your personal disclosures do not have to be detailed, and it is important to assess how members are receiving what you are sharing.

A more complete discussion of group leader self-disclosure can be found in *Groups: Process and Practice* (Corey, Corey, & Corey, 2018).

Reflection Questions

1. What are some good reasons, and not so good reasons, for being self-disclosing?
2. How do you assess what kind of therapist self-disclosure is therapeutic?
3. How might you respond if a client were to press you for personal information?
4. What are some of your own guidelines for determining the appropriateness of disclosure as a counselor?
5. What emphasis would you place on immediacy, or focusing on talking with your client about what is transpiring in your relationship with each other?

Chapter 17

Dealing With Difficult Clients

Introduction

Students are generally very interested in learning how to manage "difficult clients," and I recommend an alternative way of thinking about and approaching client resistance. If you approach your client's reluctance with understanding, patience, compassion, regard, interest, and respect, most individuals will let down their guard. Part of respecting resistance is being genuinely interested in understanding what these problematic behaviors may mean. Clients may need their defenses to survive in certain situations, and counselors should be supportive of this rather than insist that clients surrender their protection. In this chapter, I suggest that you adopt a new perspective on reframing resistance and view clients who pose challenges for you with more understanding.

• • •

*What are some ways to effectively deal with
the resistance we may encounter with clients?*

The term *resistance* often implies a lack of cooperation on the part of the client and tends to carry a negative and blaming connotation. If we perceive individuals as being resistant, we are more likely to treat them as combative and uncooperative, which tends to entrench their defensiveness. Restructure your thinking to avoid judging a client who may be anxious, cautious, guarded, frightened, or insecure. I replace the word *resistant* with *reluctant* or *ambivalent*, less judgmental terms that help me wonder about the reasons for this behavior.

Many clients will test you to determine whether it is safe to enter a relationship with you. Invite your clients to express their hesitations and anxieties, and explore your clients' experience in counseling at the initial meeting. Realize that most people will experience ambivalence and defensiveness at various times in counseling, and recognize that you can use this material to help clients take the risk of letting you know them. If you explore this ambivalence together in a respectful way, your therapeutic relationship will be strengthened and their ambivalence is likely to decrease.

In group counseling, members are motivated to change and want to be in the group but often do not know how to actively participate. Typically, awkwardness and tentativeness permeate the atmosphere as members begin to get a sense of one another. I do not view this reluctant behavior as a sign of a lack of cooperation, hostility, or stubbornness. Encouraging group participants to talk about their reluctance is often a first step toward creating a safe climate. Group members are typically anxious about not being accepted, about revealing too much about themselves, about other members not understanding them, and about fearing they will be judged. Being uncertain about what to expect in a group may heighten their anxiety and reluctance. I expect group members to be cautious about making themselves known until they feel it is safe to do so. This reluctance should be constructively explored to encourage participants to identify and acknowledge some of the factors contributing to their cautious behavior and hesitation. When members talk about their reluctance, they typically become less guarded and are more willing to become involved in meaningful work.

Reluctance to change is a normal and expected part of the therapeutic process. Although individuals may see advantages to making life changes, they also have concerns and fears about changing and often cling to the status quo. Pay attention to your reactions to these behaviors, and do your best to develop patience when working with people who are doing their best to manage their life situation.

For an interesting piece on resistance, see *Letters to a Young Therapist* (Pipher, 2003), and for ideas on how to meet resistance with acceptance, see *The Making of a Therapist* (Cozolino, 2004).

How can we most effectively deal with difficult clients?

I don't like to think in terms of "difficult clients" because this can be a shorthand way of lumping clients into a category. Avoid labeling or judging clients, and focus on behaviors that may be getting in their way of creating a productive life. Clients come to us because they are dealing with problems, and they hope we will be able to help them find solutions to these problems. We are tasked with making connections with our clients whether this is easy or more difficult. The work of counselors is often arduous, and we need to explore ways to reach clients even when they seem to be making our time with them unpleasant. When you encounter difficult clients, consider whether you might also be a difficult therapist. It takes courage to honestly look at our contribution to the relationship, which may be a key factor in the lack of progress in therapy or in our failure to connect with a client. It is not helpful to blame clients for behavior that we label resistive or problematic. I find it useful to keep in mind why a client is coming for counseling. If I can retain this perspective, I am better able to understand behavior that seems problematic.

If I am overly invested in getting clients who exhibit defensive behavior to change, I have learned that I may be overlooking my own dynamics and reactions as I interact with these individuals. My own expectations and agendas for a client may be causing a client's cautious behavior. If I am able to understand how I am being affected by certain clients, I can appropriately disclose my reactions without defensiveness. Talking about my reactions to a client's reluctance is a way to open a dialogue. I do my best to avoid criticizing the client or interpreting client reluctance as a sign of unwillingness to cooperate with the therapeutic process. It is crucial to avoid blaming either the client or myself for this reluctance. If I am protective of my ego, I lose sight of the client. In working with clients who manifest problematic behaviors, it is of the utmost importance that we recognize and deal effectively with our countertransference. My own needs and issues from my past may be getting in the way of being objective. I have found it useful to talk to a trusted colleague when I become aware that I am triggered by certain client behaviors.

Students often ask me how they can best deal with a client's anger toward them. At times, our behavior may be contributing to a client's anger. We may say or do something that is offensive to the client. In this case, our behavior has sparked anger on the part of the client, and expressing anger is a justified response to us. For example, if we are often preoccupied during therapy sessions, clients may be annoyed that we are not present with them. However, at other times, individuals may react to counselors with anger, and we may be puzzled about the reason for this. Recognize that we are probably getting more of a client's anger than we deserve. If we react too personally, we are bound to become defensive. Focus on the here-and-now interaction, and let the client know that you want to understand what is provoking the anger.

How can I respond to a client who becomes too dependent on me?

Some dependent clients will view you as all-knowing and all-wise. They will want to call you at any time of the day or night. They often expect to run over the allotted time for their sessions. They are convinced that you have the right answers for them, and they may become excessively dependent upon you to direct their lives.

If you give into the demands of these clients and take care of them, you will confirm their view that they are not capable of finding their own answers. Reflect on how much you directly or indirectly encourage their dependence on you. It is not wise to tell clients they are free to call you whenever they feel a need to do so. Of course, you want to be available to high-risk clients who may need to contact you between therapy sessions. However, if you make yourself too available, clients may come to rely on you when they should be developing other resources outside the professional relationship with you. It is important to establish and maintain boundaries with clients, both for the good of your client and for your own good.

How can counselors best react when a client offends them?

It is not helpful to become defensive when you experience offensive remarks, attitudes, or behaviors from clients. If you feel offended and find that this is getting in the way of working effectively with a client, it is generally wise to discuss what you found offensive with the client and explain how you were affected by the client's comment or behavior. It is important to suspend judgment and focus on your reactions to the offensive behavior and how this might be influencing your relationship with your client. Counselors cannot afford to have a fragile ego. If you are in supervision, consider bringing this matter into your supervision sessions and explore how this affected your ability to work with your client. A client's behavior toward you can be important material for you and your client to understand and explore in session.

What do you do if a client won't talk at all? How do you reach out to court mandated clients who are belligerent and refuse to participate?

Rather than focusing on the client's behavior, reflect on what this brings up in you. You might be telling yourself that if you were a stellar counselor your client would participate in therapy. Or you might recognize that it is difficult for you to not be appreciated for your dedication. Tuning into how you are being affected by the client's behavior doesn't take much time. Simply identify your internal reactions as a way of centering yourself before approaching your client. I often ask the client what it is like to be in this room right now, and I listen carefully before responding. The next step is to let clients know what they can expect from you, what you expect of them, how counseling works, and how you view your job as a counselor.

Do your best to get a sense of what this person is thinking and feeling about seeing you. The process of informed consent is of paramount importance in working with mandated clients, and they have a right to know what is involved in participating in therapy and if they will be penalized for not participating. Clients who are court ordered have some choice about being in the room with you, and you have the option of not agreeing to see them if they will not put forth any effort. You cannot reach clients if they dig in their heels and refuse to participate. If you listen to them with understanding, you may discover that it makes total sense for them not to trust you. They may have been betrayed by a therapist in the past, or they may be testing you to see if you are credible. Your best chance of reaching these clients is by being direct, honest, and disclosing about the counseling process. If you are working harder than your client, reflect on whether countertransference is likely to be operating, and explore this with your supervisor or another therapist.

Recommended reading for topics in this chapter include *Becoming a Helper* (Corey & Corey, 2021), *On Being a Therapist* (Kottler, 2017), and *The Secrets of Exceptional Counselors* (Kottler, 2018).

Reflection Questions

1. What associations do you have with the word "resistance"?
2. What kind of client might you find to be the most difficult for you? Why do you think this is the case?
3. Can you think of some strategies you could use to reduce defensive or resistive behavior on the part of clients?
4. What would be helpful for you in lowering your defenses if you were a client in counseling?
5. Can you think of ways of reframing resistance in more positive terms? What are some alternative ways to conceptualize and understand resistance?

Chapter 18

Supervision and Internships

Introduction

A supervised internship placement is one of the best ways to apply what you are learning in your courses to actual counseling practice. Most counselors-in-training experience anxiety when they begin seeing clients. If you approach your fieldwork and internship placements with equal parts of self-doubt and excitement, know that you are not alone. Once you become acclimated to your fieldwork placement, your self-confidence will increase as you acquire more competence. You will get the most out of your placement if you are proactive and make full use of your supervision sessions. The questions in this chapter are typical of those asked by students who often feel insecure when it comes to actually working with clients.

• • •

Can you provide graduate students in counseling with any words of wisdom or advice as we begin our internships?

Internships and supervised fieldwork placements are avenues for practical experiences that will help you become effective counselors. I advise my students to do what they can to get a placement that offers adequate supervision and where they will be able to profit from learning how to cope with the variety of problems clients bring to the agency. Your internship should provide you with a variety of settings in which to work and with various supervising environments. A wide range of opportunities exist within most agencies, so get involved in as many facets of an agency as you can. Choosing a variety of placement settings and populations enables you to discover your strengths with some populations and learn about areas of potential interest to you. Secure training in areas that are unfamiliar to you so you can acquire new knowledge and skills. The time you spend in internships and fieldwork placements provides the foundation for your future work.

Approach your internship as though it were your job. Inquire about ways to assist other staff members, especially those who have demanding positions and could use any capable help they can get. Your internship or fieldwork is one of the best ways to find out about job possibilities once you get your degree. In fact, many of my former students tell me that they were hired for an agency position where they did their internship.

How do I select the right supervisor for me and also find a good placement?

When I began my first fieldwork placement, I had no choice in the agency where I would gain experience or in who would supervise me. It never occurred to me to ask about a placement or request a particular supervisor. If I could do it again, I would have more questions and take a more active role in the process. Realistically, you may not have much choice in selecting a supervisor. During your first internship, you may be assigned a placement and a supervisor as well.

However, if you have some choice in selecting the place where you will be gaining supervised practical experience, take whatever steps you can to secure the best placement possible. Ask fellow students who have secured an internship placement about their experience in the agency. Also, specifically inquire about the supervisors at the agencies because the quality of your supervision will contribute to shaping you professionally. Talk with your faculty, and ask about the kind of experience you could get in different agencies. Do some research into agencies that interest you to find out what they can offer trainees. Explore the websites of prospective agencies and become familiar with their mission and goals, services, and internship opportunities. If you have a chance to select a supervisor, ask questions to determine what will be a productive experience for you. If you take these steps, you will be more likely to have a rewarding internship experience.

How can I best deal with supervision that is less than ideal?

The ideal supervisor may be hard to find. Supervisors in agency settings are sometimes assigned to this role with little preparation or training. Sometimes students contend that their supervisors are not competent and that their supervisory experience is inadequate. I always ask students these questions:

- How did you determine that your supervisor is not competent?
- How did you come to the conclusion that you are receiving inadequate supervision?
- Have you considered your own role in this unsatisfactory supervisory relationship?
- Have you taken the initiative to let your supervisor know what you need from supervision?

After answering these questions, you may decide that you are experiencing poor supervision. If your supervision is inadequate, be assertive in doing something about it. Take an active stance in asking for what you need from a person who could be helpful to you. If it is not practical or advisable to talk to your supervisor directly, discuss your concerns with the agency internship director or with one of your professors on campus who can give you suggestions. The best course of action may be to bring your concerns to your university supervisor. Realize that you have a right to competent supervision as a vital part of your fieldwork placement.

If it is at all possible, talk to your supervisor about what you are getting from supervision and what you would like to get that you are not getting. Avoid approaching the supervisor in a belligerent or judgmental way. Instead, talk about what you need from supervision to help you render the best services possible to your clients. Refer to what you were told to expect from supervision or refer to your supervision contract for specifics. Admittedly, there is a risk in being this candid with some supervisors, but I hope you are willing to take some calculated risks. It is important not to settle for inadequate supervision. Good supervision is vital for you to become an effective counselor.

As a graduate student, how can I maximize my supervision experience?

Your supervised fieldwork is a place to acquire knowledge and a range of new skills as you translate the theories you have learned into actual practice. You need guidance in putting your knowledge into practice. Supervision provides a forum for examining your beliefs, attitudes, personality characteristics, and behaviors as they affect your clients and the counseling process. You will get far more from your supervision experience by assuming an *active stance.* Rather than concentrating on what you cannot do, think of what you *can do* and the advantages of taking a more active role in your field placement and in your supervisory sessions. One of my colleagues who provides supervision for both master's and doctoral students recently told me how much he has learned about supervision from his supervisees. My colleague claims that he learns about effective interventions by listening to how his supervisees figure out what works well for them and their clients. Realize that many supervisors are open and interested in understanding your perspective on creating strategies that work for you.

If you are getting the most from your supervision experience, you should be able to answer these questions: What would you want to know about what is expected of you from your supervisor? What do you expect of a supervisor? How can you best prepare before each supervisory session? Think of ways to become an active supervisee, and assume a fair amount of responsibility in ensuring that your supervision is a rewarding experience. Come to each supervisory session with your questions, concerns, and successes.

I am aware that supervisees may be reluctant to share their self-doubts with their supervisor, mainly because they do not want to subject themselves to the scrutiny and criticism they fear they might receive. Supervisees can be reluctant to share any of their mistakes because they want to avoid a negative judgment. They are aware that supervisors are in an evaluative role, and supervisees often fear they will be judged incompetent if they reveal a mistake and that this will be reflected in their performance evaluation. If you have any concerns or fears about being open in your supervision sessions, I encourage you to discuss this matter with your supervisor. Taking this action is a way for you to create a trusting climate in supervision. There is a risk in being open with your supervisor, and doing this requires courage, but it is one way to enhance the working alliance you have with your supervisor. If a sense of safety has been established in this relationship, you have much to gain by bringing any self-doubts you may have into supervision and talking about interventions you tried that you determined were ineffective. If I were your supervisor, my respect for you would increase if you initiated a discussion of your concerns about either our relationship or your counseling sessions with clients. Be willing to talk about your best moments with your clients as well as the situations that did not go particularly well.

For practical recommendations for getting the most from supervision and an internship experience, see *Surviving and Thriving in Your Counseling Program* (Austin & Austin, 2020).

How can supervision be a therapeutic experience for supervisees without evolving into personal therapy?

I play multiple roles in the supervision process, functioning as a teacher, a consultant, a mentor, and occasionally as a counselor. I explain to my supervisees that I will be balancing these multiple roles and that my primary focus will be on providing a context for you to acquire counseling skills and engage in personal and professional development. I would be open to any questions you have about how these multiple roles can be balanced effectively and ethically. I would explain that clinical supervision often includes personal concerns that have an impact on your work as an intern, and I would address your personal issues to the extent that they may either impede or facilitate your ability to provide effective counseling.

Supervision is similar to therapy in some ways, but there are important differences. Supervision is a good place to identify specific aspects in your personal life that are likely to influence the quality of your professional work. However, supervision time is not meant to be devoted to the in-depth exploration of your personal problems or to deal with unfinished business from your past. Once you identify your personal issues and how they affect your work with clients, the next step is for you to seek personal therapy to explore these concerns.

For more information on supervision, see *Fundamentals of Clinical Supervision* (Bernard & Goodyear, 2019) and *Clinical Supervision in the Helping Professions: A Practical Guide* (Corey, Haynes, Moulton, & Muratori, 2021).

Reflection Questions

1. What specific steps can you take to maximize your learning from internship placements and supervision?
2. How would you go about securing a quality fieldwork or internship placement?
3. How can you better profit from your supervision? If you are not getting the quality of supervision you need, what actions could you take?
4. What would you want to know about what is expected of you by your supervisor? What do you expect of a supervisor?
5. If you became aware of personal issues that had a negative impact in your work with clients, how willing would you be to talk about this with your supervisor?

Chapter 19

Writing and Becoming a Writer

Introduction

The questions in this chapter reflect many different kinds of writing, from textbooks to your personal journal. I address questions I have been asked about writing textbooks, about my motivations for writing, about keeping a personal journal, and about writing proposals for presentations or submitting journal articles. I also discuss how it feels when a proposal is not accepted and how I have learned to challenge various forms of writer's block. Writing is a creative endeavor for elaborating on a subject of interest to you. I share my experiences with different forms of writing and suggest ways your aspirations for becoming an author can be realized.

• • •

What inspired you to begin writing textbooks?

Forty-five years ago, when I was busy teaching various undergraduate courses in human services, there were no textbooks to help me organize my courses. I began writing handouts to give to students, and these handouts eventually became chapters for a book idea. My main motivation for writing was to share ideas with my students, which is a passion that has stayed with me throughout my career.

I have been asked several times if I ever imagined that my *Theory and Practice of Counseling and Psychotherapy* textbook, first published in 1977, would become so widely used and currently appear in its 10th edition. I never imagined that my writing would be so successful over so many years. I was writing chapters for students that presented the different counseling theories in a clear, practical, and engaging style because I could not find a theory textbook in 1972 that I wanted to adopt. One day a publisher came into my office and asked, "Do you have an interest in writing a textbook?" I pulled out my student handouts and let it be known that I was excited about seeing these handouts someday become a counseling theories textbook. The publisher said that seemed like a good addition to their category of textbooks in the counseling field and that I would hear from them soon. That manuscript languished in the bottom of an editor's desk for a year before it was rediscovered and I was asked to sign a contract for the book. As I worked on the chapters for this new book, I envisioned myself talking to my students and sharing my thoughts with them about each of the theories. My teaching style has always been personal and aimed at getting students to reflect on how they can apply the material to their own life. I am pleased that this book has had a significant impact on so many students. Many students have told me that studying this book has been valuable for them personally as well teaching concepts and techniques they can draw on in their work as counselors. If you are interested in textbook writing, devote your energy to writing about subjects you are passionate about, and think of ways your writing can enhance your work in counseling practice or supervising trainees or teaching.

What suggestions do you have for those of us who have yet to write a book but are interested in doing so?

Since 2001, I have organized a panel presentation with eight writers at the American Counseling Association conferences to share information about writing a book. Some of the suggestions I offer here are gleaned from tips made by panelists on the program "Is There a Book Within You to Be Written?" There are many approaches to writing a book. We each have different schedules and different ways of working, and your writing style needs to be tailored to fit your needs and situation. Experiment until you find a style that yields the results you want. Many of you will not have sustained time to work on a book project due to pressing personal and work responsibilities. Work at your own pace, and give yourself ample time to finish the book. Schedule times you can devote your full attention to working on various stages of your book. You may need months to simply think about your topic and gather ideas that you will eventually write about. Allow yourself time to reflect and brainstorm about what your book will include.

Many people who want to write a book tell me that they get stuck and their writing stalls. I have told colleagues that they can think and plan for days or months and even spend years looking for the perfect subject, but sometimes it helps to just start writing down some thoughts and ideas and see where that leads. It may be useful to try to write something every day or on most days. If you get stuck, you can sometimes break this block by writing in an uncensored way about the experience of writing. Most people think writing a book is a grandiose and overwhelming idea, but it is OK to start small. If you write about a topic of interest to you, it may someday evolve into a book or become a smaller project that expresses your views and opinions on that topic. One thing I have learned is that writing a textbook is not finished with the first edition. Most of our books are in their 9th or 10th editions.

If you consider writing a book with a coauthor, it is extremely important that you know and respect each other, are able to commit to scheduling time to plan and write, and share similar motivations for completing a book. I have authored books as a solo venture and also engaged in collaborative writing projects with coauthors, and both have advantages and disadvantages. If you are considering collaborating with a colleague on a writing project, evaluate whether you have a good fit between you. Although you may have different perspectives on topics, you need to be unified regarding the key message of your book. Mutual respect in the coauthor relationship is essential, and it will manifest itself in the actual writing. Even if you decide not to coauthor a book with a colleague, you could find it advantageous to collaborate with colleagues on generating ideas for your writing.

What factors contribute to writing a successful book?

Writing a textbook is not a solo endeavor; it involves a team effort. I have always welcomed feedback from reviewers on my initial draft of a new manuscript or when revising a book for a new edition. Student reviewers are extremely helpful because they are the audience for textbooks, and I value what they find meaningful and helpful. Faculty members who adopt my book and have used it often are in a good position to provide ideas for revision of an existing textbook. I also engage in discussions with my colleagues on the topics I hope to cover in a book. Whether it is a new book or a revision, being open to reflecting on feedback from reviewers and others is essential. I may not agree with every suggestion, but a diversity of perspectives helps me make better decisions.

Marianne and I have coauthored five books together, and she has played a vital role in all of my books. We talk in detail about the topics before I ever do any writing. Marianne reads the manuscript at various stages of development, and she is not timid about offering critical constructive ideas about what I have written.

Having an accomplished manuscript editor is of the utmost importance in producing a successful book. We have been fortunate to have had the same copy editor for all of our new books and the multiple revisions of our textbooks for 20 years. Kay Mikel meticulously evaluates my prose and provides many insightful suggestions that result in greater clarity and a better flow for readers. A good copy editor needs to be honest and willing to make editorial changes that will improve the readability of the text, and I have learned not to be overly attached to every word I write and to consider an editor's work in an objective way.

Both Marianne and I owe a debt of gratitude to our first book editors at Brooks/Cole Publishing Company. Terry Hendrix and Claire Verduin had faith in us when we began our writing career in the mid-1970s, and they were instrumental in launching our initial books in counseling. What began with a single book soon grew into a number of textbooks in various fields of counseling. Since 2010 I have had the good fortune to work with an exceptional associate publisher, Carolyn Baker, at the American Counseling Association. My colleagues and I have produced seven books under her watchful eye, and she has guided us through the process of turning our ideas into printed books. She also played a significant role in the development of this book, *Personal Reflections on Counseling,* and consistently provided feedback and support in seeing this project to completion.

Ultimately the author is responsible for the contents of the book. However, having a publisher who has confidence in your writing is essential to creating a successful book, and many people are part of the team and contribute to the final printed work.

How has the process of writing textbooks changed since you wrote your first book?

My first book was *Teachers Can Make a Difference*, which was published in 1973. I composed chapters in handwriting on a yellow pad. I would sit by a creek in the mountains where we live, enjoy my solitude and some quiet time, and put my thoughts on paper in the hope that these words would make sense to someone. I later transitioned from pen and tablet to an Underwood typewriter, which was difficult because I had received a D in my high school typing class. It was many years later before I got my first word processor. It was a real challenge for me to learn how to use a word processor, and a fellow faculty member was kind and patient enough to teach me how to work with floppy disks!

In *Teachers Can Make a Difference*, I encouraged my students to review their personal experiences as learners and to decide how they might want to teach differently from the way they had been taught. These students were planning to become either elementary or secondary schoolteachers. Although my first book was not a bestseller and went out of print after a few years, having a book published was a turning point for me. I learned that writing a book could be a reality if I wrote about a subject I was teaching and was passionate about.

I discussed my own experiences as a learner and described the negative impact schooling had on me in this book. My elementary and high school experiences gave me a clear picture of the kind of teacher I did *not* want to be. I did everything I could to personalize student learning and to make learning interesting and personally relevant to my students' lives. My aim was to present ideas on how to teach in a way that changed lives rather than merely filling young minds with factual knowledge. I described several teachers I knew who were making a difference in the lives of students through their innovative classes. I addressed a humanistic approach to teacher education, the challenge of revolutionizing our schools, and how creative and caring teachers can make a significant difference in the lives of their students. I wanted to inspire teachers-in-training to teach in a way that had an impact on the personal lives of their students. I shared my thoughts about creating ways to personalize learning in the classroom and how to encourage students to be receptive to new ideas.

Even though I was motivated to write and blocked off time to reflect and write, becoming a writer was not a smooth process. I often struggled with getting my thoughts on paper and doubted that I had anything worthwhile to say. I had self-doubts about the value of what I was producing, but I was persistent in my efforts to share my thoughts about how teaching could be applied to the personal as well as the intellectual domain. An underlying theme of any book I have had a part in is keeping the reader clearly in mind. To this day, I still keep my audience in clear focus and think of my writing as having discussions with my students. My books have always been written for a student audience I am familiar with and about courses I have taught.

Gone are the days of sitting by a creek and developing a manuscript. The writing process today is quite different from even a decade ago due to technology. In the digital age, e-books and online programs are eclipsing print books. Currently, writing a textbook is only part of the story. Interactive programs with many different kinds of online features are in demand, and authors now devote much of their time to putting interactive packages together. I must say that even in my early years as a textbook writer I was interested in engaging readers in an active way and thinking of interactive elements within a book, and many of my textbooks were accompanied by a student manual or workbook, so perhaps I was ahead of my time in the 1970s.

Writing textbooks led to making educational videos. Video programs were produced for most of our books to help students see the practical application of the words they were reading. Several videos demonstrate individual counseling, and Marianne and I have several group counseling videos. We also have a video to bring ethical dilemmas to life by having students role-play various ways of dealing with ethical concerns. The video programs were a direct result of writing about topics and wanting to illustrate what students were reading in an action format.

Do you have suggestions about writing a proposal for a presentation at a professional conference?

I highly recommend that you attend professional conferences throughout your career. This provides opportunities to network with colleagues with interests similar to your own as well to remain current with new developments in your field. I encourage you to submit a proposal for a program, perhaps with a peer or colleague with a similar interest. Do not be deterred from attending the conference if your program proposal is not accepted. In fact, keep on submitting program proposals even if you do not get a letter saying, "Congratulations, your proposal has been accepted for the upcoming conference." Investigate the reasons your proposal was not accepted; it is essential to follow the instructions carefully and submit the proposal within the time frame provided. If your proposal is not well written, it will probably be rejected. Ask at least one colleague to review and comment on your proposal *before* you finalize it and submit it for the review process.

Keep in mind that only a small number of programs can be included at a conference. A committee typically makes selection decisions based on specific criteria. Just because your proposal is not accepted does not mean it is without merit or that you have nothing valuable to offer. The committee may simply be attempting to balance the topics offered, and sometimes too many outstanding proposals are received. I have been attending three or four professional conferences a year for more than four decades, and I generally give several presentations at most of these conventions. One year my proposal was rejected at a conference, and in the same year, two other proposals were rejected at another professional conference. The message I want to send here is to do your best when putting together a program you want to share with others. If it is accepted, that's great! But if it is not accepted, it is not the end of the story. Don't drop your membership in the organization, and do not let acceptance or rejection of a proposal determine your self-worth. Keep your motivation high, and stay focused on your goals.

Some of us are expected to write scholarly peer-reviewed articles for a professional journal. What suggestions do you have for getting journal articles accepted?

For the past 55+ years, I have authored or coauthored a number of book chapters and articles for professional journals. I would rather work on a book than devote time to writing journal articles. However, I do realize that publishing refereed articles in well-known journals is considered an essential path toward promotion in many university settings. Like program proposals for professional conferences, articles are not always accepted as submitted initially and may be returned to the author with specific suggestions for revision. Authors may react in a variety of ways to such news. Some individuals are determined to keep working on the article until they have an acceptance letter. Some interpret a nonacceptance as a personal rejection and are hesitant to continue writing. Some convince themselves that this rejection proves that they are not capable writers.

Years ago, I submitted a journal article on a topic of interest to me, and the article was rejected. I revised it three times, and each time it met with the same fate. I was excited about writing on this topic, but somehow what I wanted to share wasn't viewed as being scholarly enough. The feedback I received was that the article was too simple for most readers, that my style was too informal, that I did not follow APA style carefully, and that the article lacked a specific research base. This reinforced my belief that writers need to develop a thick skin and not take criticism too personally. Fortunately, I did not let this experience keep me from writing other journal articles. The lesson I learned was that blocking myself from considering critical feedback that could improve my writing would be counterproductive.

If you write a journal article, I hope you will not be devastated if it is not accepted on the initial round of reviews. Most people who write articles for journals typically must revise the article several times. Most journals have a quota for how many articles they can accept for publication, which means that most submissions are never published. If you do write a journal article, consider working with a coauthor to generate and exchange ideas and to help in revising the manuscript as many times as necessary. Ask other colleagues who have published articles in professional journals for suggestions on how to proceed. Be sure that the article you are writing fits the general criteria for the journal you are considering, and follow the article submission guidelines for that journal. I suggest contacting the field editor of a journal for article topic feedback. Many journals expect a scholarly piece with some research base, and if your article does not fit in this realm, chances are it will not be accepted. Remember that your worth as a person and your ability as a professional are not determined by the outcome you receive from journal editors.

How can keeping a personal journal be therapeutically beneficial?

Everything we write does not have to be published. Writing in your personal journal is meaningful even though the aim is not to have a published work. I was not required to keep a personal journal in any of the courses I took, but when I began my personal therapy in my late 20s, I started writing in my personal journal. I wrote about topics I was exploring in my individual therapy and about my reactions to what it was like for me to participate as a member in many different kinds of groups. This encouraged me to think about past events that had an impact on my present way of thinking and behaving. I did my best to write in an uncensored manner, and doing so helped me to reflect on areas I had been willing to bring into my personal therapy sessions. I have made time to read what I wrote in the past, and sometimes it is a bit disconcerting. Old patterns persisted over the years, and it became clear to me that some themes in my life were slow to change. I value the writing I did early in my career, and it has been instrumental in keeping me honest and reminding me that I am a work in progress.

I encourage students in all of my classes to write regularly in a personal journal. Even though students may have been hesitant to devote time to writing in a journal, eventually they found it immensely helpful. Reviewing their journal gave them a sense of critical choices made and areas they most wanted to target for change. My students report that devoting even a short period of time a few times each week to reflecting on how their life is going and then recording some of their thoughts and feelings is useful in providing them with an awareness of patterns in their behavior. They learn to observe what they are feeling, thinking, and doing; then they have a framework for determining the degree to which they are successfully changing old patterns and establishing new patterns that are more satisfactory.

Here are few suggestions I give students about topics to address in their journal:

- What am I learning about others and myself in this course?
- What topics were of most interest to me (and why)?
- What are the topics I most want to talk about?
- What are the topics I am avoiding talking about?

- What are some specific things I am doing in everyday life as a result of this class?
- What changes do I want to make in my attitudes, values, and behavior?
- What I am willing to do to make these changes?
- What are some obstacles I encounter in making the changes I want to make?
- What insights have I gained as a result of journal writing?

Keeping a journal is an excellent way to stimulate your personal reflections. If you are involved in your own personal counseling, your journal writing can be very useful in consolidating what you are learning and the changes you are making. If you are not in personal therapy, journal writing can be therapeutic in itself. Writing your thoughts and personal experiences in a journal could serve as the beginnings of a book that you someday may want to write.

Reflection Questions

1. If you had a book that you wanted to write, what would the title be?
2. If you decide to attend a professional conference, how inclined are you to write a proposal for a presentation? What kind of presentation would interest you?
3. Preparing articles in professional journals might be less intimidating than writing a book. If you were to write a journal article, what subject would most capture your attention?
4. What barriers get in the way of your desire to write? What are some specific ways you can use these barriers as stepping stones to success as a writer?
5. What therapeutic value do you see in writing in a personal journal? Might you consider keeping a personal journal as the seeds for a book that you may someday write?

Chapter 20

Special Topics in Counseling

Introduction

This chapter deals with a variety of questions students often raise that are basic to the practice of counseling. These topics include the role of client homework in counseling, the value of working with dreams, the effective use of metaphors, the appropriate use of humor, how to assess clients for suicidal ideation, and special concerns when working with individuals in crisis. On the business side of counseling, the topics include choosing between private practice and agency work, continuing education as a route to competence, and the value of certifications and licenses. After reading my answer to each question, spend a few moments considering whether your own answers would be similar to or different from mine.

• • •

What suggestions do you have for getting clients to carry out homework assignments?

In my early career as a high school English teacher, I was fond of giving students homework assignments, and most of my students took homework seriously. When I began to work as a counselor, I carried the idea of homework into my practice with clients. In counseling, it was important to enlist my clients as collaborators in coming up with ways to extend their learning beyond the therapy sessions and into their daily life. As a teacher, I had assigned the homework that I thought would be meaningful for my students. If I were to "assign homework" to clients without their collaboration, positive outcomes would be unlikely.

Homework is a valuable part of the change process because it enables clients to try out new behaviors in the real world. However, the term *homework* often retains negative connotations from our earlier school days. Some counselors prefer labels such as "between-session practice" or "between-session interventions." It is important for clients to have a key role in designing these activities, and it is essential that these interventions be tailored to a client's specific needs or problems. Between-session activities enable clients to practice new behaviors, test their beliefs, and try out different behaviors in daily life. These activities promote mastery and generalization of newly acquired skills in the real world. The best activities are those suggested by clients that are geared to what clients want rather than what the counselor wants for them.

In my view, much of counseling consists of educating clients, teaching them coping skills, and helping clients learn how they can continue the process of change on their own. Following up on the homework is essential. A good way to begin the next therapy session is to discuss clients' experience between sessions. I encourage clients to report on situations in which they did well and in which they experienced difficulty. Difficulty in completing homework tasks needs to be addressed. One way of doing this is by asking clients what made it difficult to complete their out-of-session assignments and what would make carrying out these tasks more realistic. Without practicing new behaviors, significant change is unlikely to occur.

What is the therapeutic value of working with dreams in counseling?

Dreams symbolize our conflicts, our wishes, and key themes in our lives. Reflecting on my own dreams has taught me the value of exploring dreams in both individual and group counseling. Although there are various ways to work with dreams, I favor the Gestalt approach to dream work in which individuals explore the meaning of their own dreams. Clients do more than simply report their dreams or talk about them. Clients are asked to bring the dream back to life, to re-create it, and to relive it as if it were happening in the present moment. Dreamers can be asked to identify with a segment of the dream and to narrate their dream from a subjective perspective. Clients may be asked to transform key elements of the dream into a dialogue and become each part of the dream. By "becoming" each of the parts of a dream as fully as possible, individuals are increasingly aware of the range of their feelings.

From the Gestalt therapy perspective, dreams contain existential messages. By avoiding analyzing and interpreting the dream and focusing instead on becoming and experiencing it in all of its aspects, individuals are able to get closer to the existential message of the dream. In working with dreams in the Gestalt style, the focus is on questions such as "What am I experiencing now?" "What was it like to recount my dream?" "What interests me most about the dream?" "What am I doing in the dream?" "What am I feeling?" "What do I want in the dream?" "What are my relationships with other objects and people in the dream?" "What is my dream telling me?" and "What am I learning about myself from my dream?"

By attending conferences on Gestalt therapy and psychodrama, I have learned how dreams can be brought to life and explored in therapy. I have come to appreciate the therapeutic value of examining my dreams, and I record my dreams in a journal. In my personal therapy, I reported some of the themes in my dreams, and I found this work to be revealing. Based on my personal work, I developed ways to tap into the meaning of dreams my clients described. As an example, here are two dreams I had some time ago, followed by some interpretations that were salient for me.

> I am at a conference, and I walk into a large room with many people. Someone tells me that I should give a presentation on group counseling. I proceed to do this, and just about everyone gets up and leaves at once. I cannot figure out why they are all leaving, except that they may be going to another program at this conference. Three people remain in the room and tell me that they thought it was rude that everyone got up and left.

In reflecting on this dream, a possible meaning is associated with my anxiety over people being interested in what I have to say at a professional conference, especially as I am aging. I have entertained self-doubts about my presentations and have had concerns about how people were receiving what I was saying. In the dream, the three people remaining could be family members (my wife and two daughters) who are sources of support.

In journaling about another dream, I became aware of concerns about my identity and in proving who I am. Some of the elements of this dream are as follows:

> I realize I lost my black wallet! I thought it might have fallen out of my left rear pocket in a taxi ride. Then I see my wallet on a table. I open my wallet, and ALL the contents are gone. Nothing is left inside my wallet.

Here are some of my associations regarding the missing contents:

Without any cash, how can I buy anything?

With my credit card gone, I cannot charge anything I may need.

I can't drive without a driver's license, and with no ID, how can I prove who I am?

How can I take care of my medical needs without my health insurance cards? If I need medical attention, I have no proof of insurance.

Without my American Counseling Association membership card, how can I prove that I am an active member of the counseling profession?

Without my American Psychological Association membership card, how can I prove that I am a psychologist?

Without my Golden Age passport, how can I get into national parks for no fee?

Without my AARP card, how can I prove that I am senior citizen, and how can I get a discount at restaurants?

Without my AAA card, what will I do if my car breaks down?

Without my little address book that lists telephone numbers, how can I call people I know?

As I reflected on this dream, and shared it with a few colleagues, it seemed obvious to me that I am concerned about my loss of identity and aging. Although I am not consciously aware of anxiety over aging, my dream seems to suggest that I am concerned about the aging process.

How can metaphors be of use in counseling?

A friend and a colleague, Patrick Callanan, taught me a great deal about paying attention to a client's metaphors. I view a metaphor as providing a glimpse into a client's story. Working with metaphors can help clients understand some aspect of the story of their life. Much like working with dreams, I do not typically interpret the meaning of a client's metaphor, but I encourage the client to reflect on what the metaphor might mean. Here are a few examples of metaphors:

> I feel like a bottomless pit.
> I bottle up all my feelings.
> I am surrounded by walls.
> I feel like a doormat.
> It feels like a hole in my soul.

I have learned to listen to how clients express themselves, both verbally and nonverbally. Metaphors can be instrumental in revealing what is going on in a client's life. For example, in a group session, Darren was talking about his early experiences growing up in his family, and in passing he said, "It feels like a hole in my soul." My coleader noted this phrase and simply said to him, "You said an important phrase. 'It feels like a hole in my soul.' Would you look at a few people and repeat that sentence?" As Darren did this, intense emotions came up for him as he experienced painful childhood memories. The group facilitators did not interpret the meaning of his sentence, but we facilitated his talking about what he was experiencing and remembering. It is therapeutic for individuals to put words to their emotions. There is a great deal of wisdom and truth expressed during moments such as these. It was important for the coleaders to carefully listen to what Darren was saying while he was emotional. At a later point, we could remind him of what he had said, and he was able then to talk about the loneliness he felt as an adolescent. We didn't give him words or tell him what to feel. As Darren talked about his early memories, he was able to gain a better understanding of the emotions he experienced.

What is the place of humor in counseling?

Counseling is a serious endeavor, but it does not have to be devoid of humor and moments of lightness. If humor is used appropriately and timed well, it can be therapeutic. Of course, humor can be misused to deflect experiencing pain or as a way to avoid confronting an unpleasant reality as well. When humor is used inappropriately, it can be counterproductive and can damage the therapeutic relationship. I have found a place for humor in the classroom, in the counselor's office, in a therapy group, and at presentations at professional conferences. In fact, when I am not finding some element of humor in my professional work, something is missing for me. I do not want to take myself too seriously, and finding humor in my foibles keeps me in touch with reality and helps keep me humble.

It is never appropriate to laugh *at* a client, but it can be therapeutic to laugh *with* a client, and a fine line distinguishes these two. For example, one of my undergraduate human service students came into my office and appeared to be emotionally shaken. When I asked him what was going on, he replied, "Yesterday my wife referred to me in very derogatory terms when she called me an asshole. I was devastated since she had never called me this before." I chuckled as he told me this, and he wondered if I was taking his situation seriously. I told him that I also have heard this comment from my wife and have learned not to let it devastate me. I also shared with him that I frequently deserve to be reminded of my annoying ways! That simple disclosure opened a discussion on how to receive hurtful comments, how to deal with conflict, and how to put difficult situations into perspective. To be sure, humor needs to be timely, engaged in sensitively, and done within the context of a trusting relationship. Years later, this student (now a colleague) reminded me of how much it meant to him when I shared a similar experience and that humor in no way detracted from our interaction. He claims that this interchange helped him learn not to take himself so seriously. In fact, he claims this was a positive turning point in our relationship.

How can I help myself stand out in the crowded field of therapists as I try to build my practice?

When it comes to business matters in the counseling profession, my knowledge is limited, so my recommendations are few. Online workshops on marketing and building a private practice are easy to access, and these programs can provide ideas for your consideration. Many of us in the counseling profession are mainly interested in the art of practicing counseling, but some business matters must be handled, such as keeping records, making client appointments, marketing for a private practice, and reaching out to colleagues in the field.

Some students are concerned that they don't know what steps to take in building a practice. If you focus on becoming the best counseling professional you can be, satisfied clients will tell their friends about you. Focus on creating excellent therapeutic relationships with clients and be willing to be your unique self. These are ways to increase the odds of standing out among others in the crowded field. Engaging in competent therapeutic work with clients is your best source of advertisement. Referrals for new clients will come to you as prior and current clients recommend you. Other ways to be recognized are to give talks in the community, to serve on community boards, to do pro bono work in a church or school, and to make connections with other therapists in your area. You don't have to compete with other good therapists; get to know them and give them opportunities to get to know you, both personally and professionally. These indirect contacts may be more effective than direct marketing strategies in ensuring that you stand out in your profession.

Is it best to work independently as a private practitioner or work for an agency where all the business part of the work is taken care of for you?

Most of my students begin their counseling career in an agency position. They are able to work with diverse client populations and to gain valuable supervised experience for a considerable time. In most agencies, the business side is taken care of by others, and you do not have to concern yourself with recruiting clients or marketing your services. The downside of this is that the pay tends to be considerably less than you would probably receive in private practice. However, working with colleagues in a community agency gives you experience in different professional roles. By beginning as a mental health provider in an agency, you can learn a great deal from your colleagues, supervisors, and clients about becoming an effective counseling practitioner. Recognize that time spent in a community agency can be a marvelous way to learn about different facets of the counseling profession. An agency perspective can be a source of learning about counseling diverse client populations, about creative ways to work with the community, and about putting your talents to use through creative projects.

Eventually some counselors may decide to establish a small private practice, perhaps working with a colleague who has an office and is willing to rent some office space to other counselors. Your colleague might be in a position to give you some referrals. Realize that there are many challenges in establishing a private practice, and gaining wide experience in agency settings could provide you with a foundation for working on your own.

For some useful suggestions for building a satisfying career, including thoughts on private practice, see Chapter 13 in *The Making of a Therapist* (Cozolino, 2004). For more information on private practice and agency practice, consider checking out these resources on the ACA website: https://aca.digitellinc. com/aca/specialties/161/view.

What has been most helpful to you in terms of continuing your education and keeping current with the times throughout the decades?

A commitment to lifelong learning is a common theme in the ethics codes of the various professional organizations as a way to maintain and enhance competence. Being a competent counselor requires participating in continuing education and being willing to obtain periodic supervision when faced with ethical, legal, or clinical dilemmas. Attending professional conferences and workshops has been extremely valuable for me, not only for increasing my knowledge of cutting-edge ideas but also for meeting and talking with colleagues. Completing a certain number of continuing education hours is required as a condition for renewal of my licensure as a psychologist. I choose to attend live presentations instead of obtaining these hours online. My aim is to keep an open mind and to be receptive to new information. In addition to accruing hours toward licensure, I use these experiences to keep up to date in both my teaching and my writing. Of course, reading journal articles and books is a pathway to ensure that I am rethinking ideas and gaining new information. I am convinced that the focus of continuing education should be on *maintaining competence* rather than simply on accumulating the required hours to maintain licensure.

The best way to form connections that will be helpful in furthering your professional ambitions is to attend professional conferences and actively seek out people in the field who share similar interests and who are doing what you want to be doing eventually. If you take the initiative in making connections with others, you are apt to find many people who are willing to share with you what they have learned in their journey. You may meet people in the field who will mentor you and provide you with support in pursuing your professional interests.

Do certifications and licenses help therapists in their profession, and are they an indication of competence?

The certification and licensing process protects counseling consumers by establishing minimum standards for professional skills and knowledge. However, I believe that training and education, along with supervised clinical experience, help counselors advance in their profession more than the certifications they acquire. Once you have a graduate degree and a professional license, you may want to pursue a specialization or seek advanced training in an area of your interest. Certifications signal that you have specialized training and possess expertise in a specific area. Contact counselors practicing in agency settings and private practice to find out what their experience was in getting certified and licensed. They can provide you with some useful tips regarding which certificates and licenses they have found valuable.

If you are interested in becoming a licensed professional counselor, you will need several thousand hours of supervised clinical experience. From the beginning of the licensure process, research your state's requirements for becoming a licensed practitioner. Many steps are involved in obtaining a license, and having guidance from others who have been through the licensure process will keep you from being overwhelmed. Just to qualify to take the examination for counselor licensure requires considerable paperwork, and you need to familiarize yourself with all of the requirements.

During the early years of my career, I viewed obtaining some symbols of proficiency (certifications and licenses) beyond my doctoral degree as a professional challenge. Obtaining licensure as a psychologist was meaningful for me, and I did feel a sense of accomplishment once I became a licensed psychologist. When I became aware that the American Board of Professional Psychology grants diplomate status to candidates who have demonstrated exceptional accomplishments in a certain field, I met all of the requirements for this award and earned the title Diplomate in Counseling Psychology (ABPP) after my name. This did not automatically make me a more competent therapist, but the award was personally meaningful. Engaging in the process to acquiring diplomate status was somewhat like climbing a professional mountain!

If you are thinking of becoming a licensed counselor, a practical guide can be found in a chapter titled "Life After Graduation" in *Surviving and Thriving in Your Counseling Program* (Austin & Austin, 2020). These authors have detailed and helpful guidelines for successfully navigating the licensure process.

How do you best assess clients who may have suicidal intentions?

Most counselors will encounter suicidal clients in their professional career, and they should be prepared to make an accurate assessment and know how to deal with clients who pose a risk for suicide. In the assessment phase, it is important to evaluate clients for depression, suicide ideation, suicide intention, suicide plans, and the presence of any risk factors associated with suicide. This assessment is especially important for clients in crisis counseling. Assess for suicidal risk at an early phase of therapy, and remain aware of any concerns during the course of therapy. Competence is of the utmost importance in the assessment of suicide and managing suicidal clients. Learn the danger signs associated with suicide. Perhaps the best single predictor of lethality is any previous attempt at suicide. Making a decision about the degree of suicidal risk is subjective and demands professional judgment. If you have limited experience in suicide assessment, do not rely on your own clinical judgment; seek consultation and supervision from professionals with experience in this area. Even experienced counselors can benefit from consultation regarding assessment and appropriate treatment when dealing with potentially suicidal individuals.

Documenting your actions is critical when counseling individuals at risk for self-harm. If a client demonstrates suicidal intent, and you do not exercise reasonable precautions, you are vulnerable to legal liability. The greatest fear of many counselors is a client's suicide. Despite your care in assessing clients' risk factors and taking appropriate actions to prevent suicide, some clients may take drastic measures to end their life. You will need to demonstrate that you took all the actions any reasonable counselor would take, including consultation.

What are some ideas for working with people who are experiencing a crisis?

Candidates for a graduate program in counseling, or interviewing for a counseling position in an agency, are often asked questions like these: "Tell us about a personal crisis you have encountered. How did you handle this crisis? What did you learn from this crisis about managing future crises of your own? Was your response effective and systematic, or were your thoughts and actions disorganized and random? How do you think that experience will either help or hinder you as a counselor working with people in crisis?" If you have worked as a counselor, think about a crisis you encountered in a counseling situation. How did you react? Did you feel that you were helpful to the client, and if so, in what ways? How might you have handled the situation better? What impact did counseling a client in a crisis situation have on you personally? How you have reacted to your own crisis situations and to intervening with clients in crisis provides a benchmark for what you are likely to do in future crises. Reflecting on your answers to these questions will help you determine what skills you need to learn to better handle your own crises and to help your clients with their crises.

Gaining competence in working in the area of crisis counseling requires coursework in crisis intervention, reading textbooks on the subject, attending workshops on crisis work, getting supervision as you begin to work with clients in crisis, and working with colleagues who have experience in this field. Competence is an issue for both new professionals and experienced counselors. Counselors often worry that they cannot do enough for clients in crisis situations. People often initiate counseling when they are in the midst of a personal crisis that is overwhelming to them. If counselors are also overwhelmed, they may lose themselves in their clients' stories and be ineffective in their work. A client who accused the counselor of not understanding her hopelessness was told that if the counselor were to share in her client's hopeless stance toward life, she would be useless to the client. A counselor's hope can eventually result in a client seeing light at the end of the tunnel and acquiring hope that life can be different.

The counselor's tasks include acknowledging what the client is facing and listening carefully to the client's story to understand the client's perspective. We also need to make an assessment of the client's immediate situation and discover what coping resources are available. Our willingness to be present for and to connect with others as they attempt to put their lives back together can be healing. During our first meeting with a client in crisis, we can give the gift of presence by what we say and by reflecting genuine caring, a sense of hope for the future, a deep sense of compassion, and a willingness to suggest resources to help them cope with what they are going through. Presence is powerful and often transcends what we may be able to do to change the situation.

To learn more about crisis counseling, see *Crisis Intervention Strategies* (James & Gilliland, 2017), *A Guide to Crisis Intervention* (Kanel, 2018), and *Coping Skills for a Stressful World: A Workbook for Counselors and Clients* (Muratori & Haynes, 2020).

Reflection Questions

1. What value do you place on homework in counseling? What are your thoughts about how you would present homework to your clients?
2. How can you best assess your level of competence? Once you acquire competence in a specific area, what can you do to maintain your competence?
3. What role do you think humor should play in therapy relationships? How can you assess the appropriateness of humor and the impact it has on a client?
4. What concerns do you have regarding the assessment process for suicidality risk?
5. How do you think your personal experiences with crisis situations would influence your ability to work effectively with clients who are in crisis?

Epilogue

Writing this book has given me an opportunity to review significant turning points in my career and to clarify what I have learned personally and professionally. My career path has been marked by many twists and turns. I have followed my interests, pursued my passions, and chosen to take on promising opportunities throughout my career.

I typically adopt a personal style of writing, and this is one of my most personal books. I have responded here to many questions students have asked me over the years. My disclosures about lessons I have learned and descriptions of how I struggled during my graduate school days and early career may assist you in discovering multiple pathways toward achieving your life goals and professional ambitions. I hope this conversation provides you with some new ideas to think about as you chart your own career in counseling.

In reflecting on my 60-year career in teaching and my involvement in the counseling profession, I have become aware of how much more complex life is today than it was when I was a graduate student and when I began teaching in 1961. As students today, you have many more resources than I had and are exposed to coursework far beyond anything I could have imagined in my graduate counseling program. I have been part of this changing landscape over these many years as the education and training of those in the helping professions has expanded to meet the needs that have been recognized by those who provide a variety of services. Significant developments in our society have encouraged the counseling discipline to delve deeply into areas such as professional ethics, best practices in counseling, multicultural factors that influence counseling practice, the role of clinical supervision, understanding and working with many aspects of diversity, and recognizing the role of social and environmental factors in understanding human problems.

I have come to increasingly appreciate the character of today's students in both undergraduate and graduate programs in counseling and social work. You have a clear vision for working toward a better future and are truly motivated to address the ills in society. Whether you are counseling individuals or working with groups in the community, you are dedicated to creating ripples in a pond that will spread beyond your work with one individual or community. I believe my students are highly motivated to become excellent counselors, and my contacts with university students from many regions in the United States and internationally strengthen my optimistic view of these emerging new leaders. At the professional conferences I attend each year, I encounter counseling students who fill me with hope for the future of the profession. These young professionals are eager to learn, want to make a difference, are doing their own personal work, and are getting involved in various forms of social action.

I imagine that many readers of this book are in graduate training programs or are new professionals in the counseling field. I have emphasized throughout this book that self-care is essential to your success in this profession and in life. Taking care of yourself physically, psychologically, mentally, socially, and spiritually is not a selfish pursuit. Positive self-care is required for each of us if we hope to provide care for others. I urge you to establish a self-care plan and to revisit this as it and you evolve throughout your career. By enriching our own lives, we build a reservoir of energy that we can tap into in helping others find their own way to a more fulfilling life.

You are on a journey toward becoming an exceptional counselor. In pursuit of that goal, consider these factors. The coursework you are doing is crucial in acquiring competence, but realize that knowledge and skills alone are not sufficient. If you are striving for excellence, you need to be willing to work on yourself as a person. If you have been or currently are in personal counseling, examine the qualities your therapist has shown that engendered trust and confidence in you as a client. Is it the theory to which your therapist adheres? The techniques your therapist employs? Or the degrees and licenses your counselor has hanging on the wall? It is unlikely that any of these attributes have cemented the effective therapeutic relationship between you. Rather, your trust has depended on the capacity of your counselor to establish a caring and challenging therapeutic relationship with you. Your personal qualities are the essential tools in creating an effective therapeutic relationship and in becoming an exceptional counselor.

I encourage you to entertain your dreams and not to limit your vision. Be willing to work diligently to turn your dreams into reality. Have the courage to challenge your fears so they do not stop you from pursuing your dreams. You will make mistakes along the way, so be willing to acknowledge these missteps and be open to learning from them. Becoming the person you want to be and becoming a competent professional entail work and striving toward your goals, but you will collect rewards along the way that help you feel that your work is worthwhile.

You are not alone in your journey toward becoming a professional counselor. Be willing to reach out to friends, peers, professors, and mentors to find the support you need and advice you can use at each crossroad in your path. Seek out at least one mentor who can help you achieve your academic goals and reach your professional ambitions. Imagine the legacy you would like to create, and identify the steps you can take now toward achieving this legacy. Trust yourself to become a competent counselor who will make a key difference in the lives of those with whom you work.

I suggest that you take some time now to review the Reflection Questions at the end of each chapter. Thinking and writing about your answers to those questions is a good way to maximize the personal benefit of this book. I have enjoyed writing this book, and I sincerely hope you enjoy reading and reflecting on the messages I have conveyed. This book will have served its purpose if I have encouraged you to apply these messages in your own unique way to both your personal life and your professional work.

• • •

References and Recommended Readings

American Counseling Association. (2014). *ACA code of ethics.* Alexandria, VA: Author.

Austin, J. A., & Austin, J. T. (2020). *Surviving and thriving in your counseling program.* Alexandria, VA: American Counseling Association.

Bernard, J. M., & Goodyear, R. K. (2019). *Fundamentals of clinical supervision.* Upper Saddle River, NJ: Pearson.

Cashwell, C. S., & Young, J. S. (Eds.). (2020). *Integrating spirituality and religion into counseling* (3rd ed.). Alexandria, VA: American Counseling Association.

Corey, G. (1973). *Teachers can make a difference.* Columbus, OH: Charles E. Merrill.

Corey, G. (2010). *Creating your professional path: Lessons from my journey.* Alexandria, VA: American Counseling Association.

Corey, G. (2016). *Theory and practice of group counseling* (9th ed.). Boston, MA: Cengage Learning.

Corey, G. (2019). *The art of integrative counseling* (4th ed.). Alexandria, VA: American Counseling Association.

Corey, G. (2021). *Theory and practice of counseling and psychotherapy* (Enhanced 10th ed.). Boston, MA: Cengage Learning.

Corey, G., Corey, M. S., Callanan, P., & Russell, J. M. (2015). *Group techniques* (4th ed.). Belmont, CA: Brooks/Cole, Cengage Learning.

Corey, G., Corey, M. S., & Corey, C. (2019). *Issues and ethics in the helping professions* (10th ed.). Boston, MA: Cengage Learning.

Corey, G., Corey, M. S., & Haynes, R. (2014). *Groups in action: Evolution and challenges, DVD and workbook* (2nd ed.). Belmont, CA: Brooks/Cole, Cengage Learning.

Corey, G., Corey, M. S., & Haynes, R. (2015). *Ethics in action: DVD and workbook* (2nd ed.). Belmont, CA: Brooks/Cole, Cengage Learning.

Corey, G., Corey, M. S., & Muratori, M. (2018). *I never knew I had a choice* (11th ed.). Boston, MA: Cengage Learning.

Corey, G., Haynes, R., Moulton, P., & Muratori, M. (2021). *Clinical supervision in the helping professions: A practical guide* (3rd ed.). Alexandria, VA: American Counseling Association.

Corey, G., Muratori, M., Austin, J. T., & Austin, J. A. (2018). *Counselor self-care.* Alexandria, VA: American Counseling Association.

Corey, M. S., & Corey, G. (2021). *Becoming a helper* (8th ed.). Boston, MA: Cengage Learning.

Corey, M. S., Corey, G., & Corey, C. (2018). *Groups: Process and practice* (10th ed.). Boston, MA: Cengage Learning.

Cozolino, L. (2004). *The making of a therapist.* New York, NY: Norton.

Herlihy, B., & Corey, G. (2015a). *ACA ethical standards casebook* (7th ed.). Alexandria, VA: American Counseling Association.

Herlihy, B., & Corey, G. (2015b). *Boundary issues in counseling: Multiple roles and responsibilities* (3rd ed.). Alexandria, VA: American Counseling Association.

Hill, C. E. (2018). *Meaning in life: A therapist's guide.* Washington, DC: American Psychological Association.

James, R. K., & Gilliland, B. E. (2017). *Crisis intervention strategies* (8th ed.). Boston, MA: Cengage Learning.

Johnson, R. (2013). *Spirituality in counseling and psychotherapy: An integrative approach that empowers clients.* Hoboken, NJ: Wiley.

Johnson, W. B., & Ridley, C. R. (2018). *The elements of mentoring* (3rd ed.). New York, NY: St. Martin's Press.

Kabat-Zinn, J. (2018). *The healing power of mindfulness: A new way of being.* New York, NY: Hachette Books.

Kanel, K. (2018). *A guide to crisis intervention* (6th ed.). Boston, MA: Cengage Learning.

Kolmes, K. (2017). Digital and social media multiple relationships on the Internet. In O. Zur (Ed.), *Multiple relationships in psychotherapy and counseling: Unavoidable, common, and mandatory dual relations in therapy* (pp. 185–195). New York, NY: Routledge/Taylor & Francis.

Kottler, J. A. (2017). *On being a therapist* (5th ed.). New York, NY: Oxford University Press.

Kottler, J. A. (2018). *The secrets of exceptional counselors*. Alexandria, VA: American Counseling Association.

Lee, C. C. (Ed.). (2018). *Counseling for social justice* (3rd ed.). Alexandria, VA: American Counseling Association Foundation.

Lee, C. C. (Ed.). (2019). *Multicultural issues in counseling: New approaches to diversity* (5th ed.). Alexandria, VA: American Counseling Association.

Maslach, C. (2015). *Burnout: The cost of caring* (2nd ed.). Los Altos, CA: Malor Books.

Meichenbaum, D. (2012). *Roadmap to resilience: A guide for military, trauma victims and their families*. Clearwater, FL: Institute Press.

Muratori, M., & Haynes, R. (2020). *Coping skills for a stressful world: A workbook for counselors and clients*. Alexandria, VA: American Counseling Association.

Neff, K. (2011). *Self-compassion*. New York, NY: William Morrow/HarperCollins.

Neff, K., & Germer, C. (2018). *The mindful self-compassion workbook*. New York, NY: Guilford Press.

Norcross, J. C., & Goldfried, M. R. (Eds.). (2019). *Handbook of psychotherapy integration* (3rd ed.). New York, NY: Oxford University Press.

Norcross, J. C., & Lambert, M. J. (Eds.). (2019). *Psychotherapy relationships that work: Evidence-based therapist contributions* (Vol. 1, 3rd ed.). New York, NY: Oxford University Press.

Norcross, J. C., & VandenBos, G. R. (2018). *Leaving it at the office: A guide to psychotherapist self-care* (2nd ed.). New York, NY: Guilford Press.

Norcross, J. C., & Wampold, B. E. (Eds.). (2019). *Psychotherapy relationships that work: Evidence-based responsiveness* (Vol. 2, 3rd ed.). New York, NY: Oxford University Press.

Pipher, M. (2003). *Letters to a young therapist*. New York, NY: Basic Books.

Reamer, F. G. (2017). Multiple relationships in a digital world: Unprecedented ethical and risk management challenges. In O. Zur (Ed.), *Multiple relationships in psychotherapy and counseling: Unavoidable, common, and mandatory dual relations in therapy* (pp. 196–206). New York, NY: Routledge/Taylor & Francis.

Remley, T. P., & Herlihy, B. (2020). *Ethical, legal, and professional issues in counseling* (6th ed.). Boston, MA: Pearson.

Scherger, J. E. (2019). *Lean and fit: A doctor's journey to healthy nutrition and greater wellness* (3rd ed.). [Self-published]. CreateSpace Independent Publishing Platform.

Stebnicki, M. A. (2017). *Disaster mental health counseling: Responding to trauma in a multicultural context.* New York, NY: Springer.

Sue, D. W., Sue, D., Neville, H. A., & Smith, L. (2019). *Counseling the culturally diverse: Theory and practice* (8th ed.). Hoboken, NJ: Wiley.

Webber, J. M., & Mascari, J. B. (Eds.). (2018). *Disaster mental health counseling: A guide to preparing and responding* (4th ed.). Alexandria, VA: American Counseling Association Foundation.

Wheeler, A. M., & Bertram, B. (2019). *The counselor and the law: A guide to legal and ethical practice* (8th ed.). Alexandria, VA: American Counseling Association.

Wubbolding, R. E. (2017). *Reality therapy and self-evaluation: The key to client change.* Alexandria, VA: American Counseling Association.

Yalom, I. D. (1997). *Lying on the couch: A novel.* New York, NY: Perennial.

Yalom, I. D. (2003). *The gift of therapy.* New York, NY: Perennial.

Zur, O. (2007). *Boundaries in psychotherapy: Ethical and clinical explorations.* Washington, DC: American Psychological Association.

Zur, O. (Ed.). (2017). *Multiple relationships in psychotherapy and counseling: Unavoidable, common, and mandatory dual relations in therapy.* New York, NY: Routledge/Taylor & Francis.